# PRAYING IN GOD'S WILL

## MORGAN KIZER

WESTBOW
PRESS®
A DIVISION OF THOMAS NELSON
& ZONDERVAN

This book is a work of non-fiction. Unless otherwise noted, the author and the publisher make no explicit guarantees as to the accuracy of the information contained in this book and in some cases, names of people and places have been altered to protect their privacy.

WestBow Press books may be ordered through booksellers or by contacting:

WestBow Press
A Division of Thomas Nelson & Zondervan
1663 Liberty Drive
Bloomington, IN 47403
www.westbowpress.com
844-714-3454

Cover art provided by Ella Fortenberry, a high school student at Carmel Christian School, Matthews, North Carolina.

Unless otherwise indicated, scripture quotations are taken from the ESV Bible® (The Holy Bible, English Standard Version®), copyright © 2001 by Crossway Bibles, a publishing ministry of Good News Publishers. Used by permission. All rights reserved.

Scripture quotations marked KJV are taken from the King James Version.

ISBN: 978-1-6642-9366-3 (sc)
ISBN: 978-1-6642-9365-6 (e)

Print information available on the last page.

WestBow Press rev. date: 04/29/2023

# ACKNOWLEDGEMENTS

WHILE I TAKE PERSONAL RESPONSIBILITY FOR ALL ERRORS AND SHORTCOMINGS, I OWE A DEBT OF GRATITUDE TO MY FRIENDS, ROBERT E. BISHOP, MICHAEL S. FREEMAN, LAWSON HUNTLY, MICHAEL J. TARILLION, AND ALICE CRANE YOTHERS, WHO SPENT TIME AND EFFORT HELPING ME WITH THEIR ADVICE, SUGGESTIONS AND ENCOURAGEMENT. WITHOUT THEIR INPUT THIS BOOK WOULD BE FAR LESS WORTHY OF YOUR CONSIDERATION.

# DEDICATION

This book is dedicated to E.R. (Sarge) Grey who was the chaplain at LeTourneau Collage. He was a good example of what a Christian should be.

# CONTENTS

# PREFACE

Prayer is a wonderful privilege. It is both simple and complex. Ask yourself, "How many leaders and people of importance can you communicate with any time day or night that have the ability to provide instant heartfelt personal help?" Whereas a believer can communicate with the all-knowing, all-powerful Creator of the universe at any time and discuss anything. A believer who is truly communicating with the Father can reasonably expect Him to produce life changing events for the benefit of those who have sincerely ask for His help.

As you read this book you will notice several reoccurring thymes. They are repeated for a reason. THEY ARE VERY IMPORTANT! Without them you are just talking into a cell phone that doesn't have any batteries. NOTE 1: There are a few places where I have inserted 4 periods (....). When you see them stop and think seriously about what you just read. These statements need to be understood and digested thoroughly!

I have tried to make this book as Biblical and as practical as possible. Many times I have inserted my own thoughts. Take them for what you think they are worth. However, if you choose to ignore any of God's Word, you are doing so at your own loss.

To some extent I have tried to make each chapter concise so it can be read quickly for people who happen to notice an interesting topic. One can normally read a short chapter while browsing in a bookstore. On the other hand, I have had to make a few chapters longer because of the nature of their content.

Hopefully, you will choose to immerse yourself in The Holy Bible. It contains everything spiritual that you will ever need to know. If you do this under the leadership of the Holy Spirit you will never regret it.

None of us are perfect. Should you find errors please, forgive me. No earthling has every facet of Scripture 100% right.

It is my sincere prayer that you will follow the leading of the Holy Spirit in all that you read and all that you do.

Morgan Kizer

**"And so, from the day we heard, we have not ceased to pray for you, asking that you may be filled with the knowledge of his will in all spiritual wisdom and understanding, so as to walk in a manner worthy of the LORD, fully pleasing to him, bearing fruit in every good work and increasing in the knowledge of God. May you be strengthened with all power, according to his glorious might, for all endurance and patience with joy, giving thanks to the Father, who has qualified you to share in the inheritance of the saints in light. He has delivered us from the domain of darkness and transferred us to the kingdom of his beloved Son, in whom we have redemption, the forgiveness of sins."**

Colossians 1:9-14 KJV

Prayer is not reciting
a series of magic words
that cause things to happen!

God is sovereign! He can
do anything that
He chooses to do. The Holy
Bible mentions some of the
answers that He has already
pre-determined. He is consistent
and does everything in agreement
with His written Word.

God is perfect. If He were to change
He would be other than perfect!

# CHAPTER 1

# INTRODUCTION

## STEP ONE

WHO DO WE THINK WE are? We humans are a conflicted bunch. We have many habitual failings, yet we keep trying to convince ourselves that we are better than just being okay and that somehow we deserve more than what we have. Many of us act as if we should be rewarded for just existing. Oftentimes, even when we know something can't work or is not good for us, we just keep on doing it. We often form less than acceptable prayer habits and over time we become comfortable with them. Somehow, we never seem to learn. For us, conflicts and failures seem to be a natural part of life. We pray and nothing seems to happen. Failure should never be acceptable or normal for a true believer!

Hey wait a minute. I thought this was a book about prayer. It is. But first there are a few things we need to get straight before we are ready to study prayer. Why would anyone choose to listen to us; much less give us meaningful help in important life matters?,

All over the world there are people who pray. Unfortunately, many are not true believers. In fact, it would be difficult to find a religion or even a cult that did not have some form of prayer. Most people instinctively seek supernatural intervention and guidance for their lives. Some are desperate. They are hoping that a divine being will in some way promote their happiness and wellbeing or save them from an imminent disaster or the well-deserved consequences of their behavior.

Some people have an edge here. Those who have been convicted of their wrongdoings (sins) and have asked the Creator of the universe to forgive and save them from their default fate of never-ending punishment are in a good position for positive result filled answers to their prayers.

An individual is a believer if he believes the Holy Bible. It states that God will save anyone who sincerely ask for His forgiveness and trust only in Jesus for his redemption (Romans 10:9-10 &13). Once a person has come this far, they have many valid and wonderful prayer opportunities. Everyone else has only two options:

1. Everlasting punishment, not a good choice.
2. Asking Jesus to forgive and save them from a well-deserved fate of everlasting punishment. (Becoming a true believer in Christ.)

This book is for those who have opted out of the universal default fate of everlasting punishment by accepting God's free gifts of forgiveness and salvation. This book is written only for believers.

All believers have problems. We still have our earthly desires and wants, but we also have a Savior who loves us very much. However, being a believer does not automatically provide us with an endless get-out-of-jail free card. There are always negative earthly consequences for bad thoughts and behaviors.

Becoming a believer does in fact give a person a new set of responsibilities. The good LORD expects each of His followers to live a holy life (Leviticus 20:7). Being saved presents the believer with standards and behavior obligations that only a Holy God could rightfully require.

A holy life is not free from pain, struggle, or problems. It is in these challenges where believers are enabled to demonstrate the differences that Christ has made in their lives. This is also where most of us have difficulties. We want, no, we expect happiness and a life full of blessings. We didn't expect a life of struggles and conflicts. Hey wait a minute. I don't like this. I just want to get my prayers answered. I want a better life. Calm down. We will get there; but first we need to get our minds right. God is not Santa Clause! It is his number one desire for each of us to be more like Jesus. More than anything else, He wants each of us to be HOLY!

Jesus did not have an easy life. If we are going to be like him, we should not expect anything different. YUCK! But, but, nothing. God wants us to be holy. But I thought that God wants us to be happy. He does. But I thought that God wants us to have a good life. He does. Wait a minute. Something doesn't seem right. Something is wrong. It certainly is! If we don't understand what's wrong, then how can we expect to get it fixed?

The confusion factor that we need to understand is that each of us has a sin nature. Yes, even the best of good believers. When Christ saved us, He did not remove the compulsion to sin from our hearts. Instead, He gave us an additional new nature. The new nature and our old sin nature are in constant war with each other. Our old nature is self-centered. It strives toward us having everything that we desire right now in contrast to our new nature that draws us toward personal holiness and leads us into doing God's will (Paul had the same problem with his old nature that we do.) See (Romans 7:14-25). Believers are constantly having battles between their two natures.

Unbelievers have a different life. They want what they want, and their most imperative factor is how to get it with the least amount of effort and when they get what they thought that they wanted, then they repeat the cycle of desiring one more obsession after another.

Sadly, the average believer's prayer life has many prayers that are spoken from the vantage point of their old sinful nature. Request for more stuff, better stuff, achieving personal status, and victories in life's petty arguments. Whereas, our new nature would have us making more requests for personal victories over temptation, for the gospel to be presented to the lost, for their salvation, and for personal holiness.

The war between the two natures does not end when we pray. The old sin nature will even push good believers toward making request for their wants and will encourage them to rationalize that somehow they expect God to alter His Devine plans for their spiritual improvement and happiness. Some "Christians" even believe that they deserve special earthly rewards. Many act as if they would rather have a mud hut now at the expense of having a permanent golden mansion, later on.

Here-in is a major prayer problem. Believers must be constantly on guard to identify and intercept any thoughts or actions that are promoted by their old sinful nature. Yes, even in prayer. Victory is only possible by completely and joyfully submitting to God's Holy Spirit! Any of us can make this decision but we can only carry it out by submitting minute by minute to the help, leading, and filling of the Holy Spirit.

No one is personally strong enough to become holy or even semi-holy by his own efforts. We humans have often tried and we always fail. We really can't help ourselves. Until a person surrenders to follow God's Holy Spirit minute by minute, he will wrestle on and on in endless struggles. It is just as if we were taking a case to court. We must have proper standing before we can accomplish anything.

If anyone is to get an audience with the Almighty, he will first have to pray two special prayers: The first prayer is to ask God to save him from his well-deserved fate of eternal punishment and for the forgiveness of his sins. NOTE 1: it is not a matter of repeating the correct prayer words that saves a person, all prayers must be truly heartfelt. (The becoming a Christian prayer needs to be prayed only once.) NOTE 2: All prayers must be sincere and honest, otherwise they don't count!)

> **"That if thou shalt confess with thy mouth
> the LORD Jesus, and believe in
> thine heart that God hath raised him
> from the dead, thou shalt be saved."**
>
> Romans 10:9KJV

This is God's requirement. This is the prayer that completes the transformation of a person into a believer.

The words of the second prayer are similar to the first prayer. In this prayer a person, who is already a believer, asks God to forgive him of his newly committed sins. The object of this prayer is to restore fellowship with the Father. When this is done the he is ready to pray about any other needs and concerns.

## STEP TWO

In step 1 we address the letter to our Father who is in Heaven. In step 2 we put the stamp of the Holy Spirit on our letter. Real prayer is talking to the Creator of the universe, the LORD God Almighty. This is an awesome privilege. Pause for a moment and think about this. As unworthy as we know we are, He has allowed us into His Throne Room. He is listening to every word we speak. He has infinite power. He can do anything! ….

This is in sharp contrast to the way most of us pray. We often regard the Almighty as some kind of divine errand boy. We give him an assignment list and expect Him to give us prompt and courteous service. It is because of His intense love that He hasn't instantly vaporized us. We wouldn't dare address an earthly ruler this way. When we pray, we should first stop and consider to whom we are talking. Our heavenly Father understands our condition and our needs. Jesus's disciples had similar concerns. They asked Him, "How should we pray"? The Bible provides us with His guidelines for prayer.

**"Now Jesus was praying in a certain place, and when he finished, one of his disciples said to him. "LORD, teach us to pray, as John taught his disciples." And he said to them, "When you pray, say: "Father, hallowed be your name. Your kingdom come. Give us each day our daily bread, and forgive us our sins, for we ourselves forgive everyone who is indebted to us. And lead us not into temptation."**

Luke 11:1-4

NOTE 3: The very first specification in Jesus's instructions on how to pray is to pray to the Father. If praying to the Father wasn't important, then why did He put it first in His instructions list? Our only access to the Father is through Jesus. The Holy Spirit's part is to interpret our prayers to the Father. The entire trinity is involved when a believer prays. Believers should respect each one by not misdirecting their prayers or disrespecting their different functions.

In Matthew chapter 6 Jesus provides some additional detailed instructions:

1. Vs. 5 **"And when you pray, you must not be like the hypocrites. For they love to stand and pray in the synagogues and at the street corners, that they may be seen by others. Truly, I say to you, they have received their reward."** Pray privately.

2. Vs. 6 **"But when you pray, go into your room and shut the door and pray to your Father who is in secret. And your Father who sees in secret will reward you."** Pray secretly.

3. Vs. 7 **"And when you pray, do not heap up empty phrases as the Gentiles do, for they think they will be heard for their many words."** Pray honestly and concisely.

4. Vs. 8 **"Do not be like them, for your Father knows what you need before you ask him."** When you pray you don't need to provide the Father with a detailed list of your desires, but you are free to express them.

5. Vs. 9-13 **"Pray then like this: Our Father in heaven, hallowed be your name. Your kingdom come, <u>Your will be done</u>, on earth as it is in heaven. Give us this day our daily bread, and forgive us our debts, as we also have**

**forgiven our debtors. And lead us not into temptation, but deliver us from evil.**" Pray earnestly for God's Will to be done above everything else.

6. Vs. 14-15 **"For if you forgive others their trespasses, your heavenly Father will also forgive you, but if you do not forgive others of their trespasses, neither will your Father forgive your trespasses."** There is a steep penalty if you fail to forgive others for the things that they have done to you. Could this be the reason your forgiveness prayers feel so unanswered. Is this why you continue to feel guilty even after you have voiced many forgiveness prayers?

These are some of God's key instructions for believers who desire to pray good effective prayers. NOTE 4: There are many other prayer teachings woven throughout the Bible. Believers have the responsibility to read, study and follow each of them. If you don't have the desire to study God's Word, then something is seriously wrong!

**"Study to shew thyself approved unto God,
a workman that needeth not to be ashamed,
rightly dividing the word of truth"**

II Timothy 2:15KJV

Everyone who has been brought up attending church has also heard the many prayers of the most righteous people that they know: pastors, deacons, elders, Sunday school teachers, and some very devout believers. Mixed in with them are the prayers of many other believers and perhaps even a few non-believers. NOTE 5: Non-believers have only one legitimate prayer (Romans 10:13 paraphrased): "LORD, please forgive me and save me from my sins". However, nothing is as simple as it may first seem. There are people, including many respectable church members, who haven't honestly asked Jesus to: save them, though they may have repeated the words contained in a salvation prayer. NOTE 6: A prayer that is not honest never reaches the Father. Just **repeating a special set of words will not save anyone**! The key to understanding this is found in (Romans 10:9 KJV) Where it includes this as a condition for a salvation prayer: "...**believe in thine heart** ...". **When a person definitely says something and knows that it is untrue it is a lie.** This is illustrated further in (Acts chapter 5) in the story of Ananias and Sapphira. They lied to the Holy Ghost and promptly died because they had lied to God. God didn't design any of us to be parrots. Taken very literally, if you don't mean what you are saying, then you are lying! NOTE 7: You can fix this any time you choose in less than one minute!

NOTE 8: There are people who are not believers, they haven't actually trusted Christ for their salvation; but they have been deceived by Satan into thinking that they, too, are Christians. Many of these rationalize that they have been brought up in a Christian community. Some of these have joined a church and think that they are as good as anybody else. (NOTE 9: **Salvation is not based on good works (being good). This belief is common and is also a false belief!!!....)**

> "For by grace you have been saved through
> faith. And this is not your own
> Doing: it is the gift of God, not a result of
> works, so that no one may boast."

Ephesians 2:8-9

The people who believe that they are saved by being good are rightfully identified as being apostate. Sooner or later their true allegiance will be revealed.

Think about a person whose spouse treats them badly. After

they abuse them, they will often try to get back into the good graces of their spouse. They will often say that they are sorry. VERY SORRY! ....

Many times, appropriate words are not truly meant. And so it is with some prayers, when they're not meant, they're not sent.

At the very best, the concepts and guidelines you read about in this book can only serve to wet your spiritual appetite. There is no substitute for a person devoting time and sweat and sometimes tears into reading and studying God's Word and maintaining a substantial, honest prayer relationship with the good LORD.

# CHAPTER 2

# INEFFECTIVE PRAYERS

**"And when you pray, do not heap up empty
phrases as the Gentiles do, for they think that
they will be heard for their many words."**

Matthew 6:7

THERE ARE SOME PRAYERS THAT the Good LORD will not answer. They are so inappropriate that they don't belong in His Throne Room. This is because the Holy Spirit filters and translates all prayers so that they correctly express our true thoughts.

**"Likewise the Spirit helps us in our weakness.
For we do not know what to pray for as we
ought, but the Spirit himself intercedes for
us with groanings too deep for words."**

Romans 8:26

Some prayers are so lacking in substance that they seemingly end up in the "trash bin" (James 4:3). Unfortunately, this can leave people, who don't understand prayer, in a deeper level of skeptical unbelief. They prayed as hard as they could for a new Lamborghini and some were even willing to let God select the color. These people have spiritual delusions. They need to repent and go back to square one.

Another ineffectual prayer is the "pray for everything and everybody" prayer. Some people may be pleased when a child prays it, but it is not a prayer for a mature believer. While it is good for a Christian to pray for all the people in a disaster area, it is better for them to ask God to spiritually energize the believers who are extending their witness to them by personally helping and showing them true Christian compassion in their moment of need.

One of the major problems that many believers have is that they often decide what the Almighty needs to do in a given situation and then they assign the task of making it happen to Him. While this prayer may be well intended it denigrates the Almighty. He is all knowing, all wise and all powerful and He knows much better than we do what needs to be done. A far better prayer would be for the believer to express his concerns and to ask his loving heavenly Father to help and to use him as He sees fit and that His will is done. NOTE 1: There is nothing better than God's Will! .... Any prayer that is less than that is second-rate. If you have fears about trusting Him You need to think about and address these fears. Where did they come from? Who sent them? Why were they sent to you? Do they prevent or hinder you from doing God's will?

Fortunately for us the Holy Spirit intercepts all our prayers and interprets them to the Father. He takes our less-than-ideal prayers and conveys the correct messages to the Father. Too often the best translation of our prayers is unanswerable.

Generally speaking, an ineffectual prayer is any prayer or Divine requests that are outside of God's will. This clear statement generates another question, "How do we know what is in God's will and what is outside of His will?" The simple and often-overlooked Sunday school answer is that we should read the Bible and follow its instructions. While this is technically correct, it doesn't offer much help for someone who is in a bad emergency situation, who currently doesn't have a Bible, or in his present circumstances doesn't have the time or ability to read and study it. This is one of the reasons for this book. This could be one of your reasons for reading it. Hopefully, there will be sufficient spiritual instruction so that you can get on the right path.

All of us need help with our prayers. A confirmation of this is available with a quick answer to a single diagnostic question: "What percentage of your prayers are clearly answered in the affirmative?"

You prayed for something and you got it. Any answer that is less than a high percentage indicates a serious spiritual problem? Don't let this get you down. After all, by reading this you are demonstrating that you want to improve your prayer life. Prayer is not a wish list. A prayer may mention some things that you want but their expression should always be in the context of wanting God's will to be done above everything else.

I have researched the Scriptures and have founded some of the key things that a believer can and should pray for. Are you motivated enough to make a few changes? What is it worth to you to get more of your prayers answered? Are you willing to stop seeking something that you want in order to obtain something much better that will last forever? When you think about the thing you don't want to give up which part of your nature is influencing you? Your old nature or your new nature? When you can sincerely answer this question, you are ready to read the next chapter. ....

# CHAPTER 3

# WHAT SHOULD I PRAY ABOUT

Believers should pray about everything and everyone that the Holy Spirit puts on their heart! Phrased another way, what are some of the topics that God's Spirit normally puts on a believer's heart? Some of them are listed below in the order that I believe that they should be addressed. When the Spirit moves you otherwise, ignore my suggestions.

Some topics are universal and every believer should be praying about them on a regular basis. Others are event based. NOTE 1: there are good reasons for constantly repeating some prayers. Everyone has a lower nature and it pops up ever so often, even in the best of us. It is similar to driving a nail. You need to keep on pounding until it is driven to its final resting place. The following prayer sequence is suggested; but pray in the way that God's Spirit leads you.

1. Forgiveness of sins/confession - Everyone sins (Romans 3:23), yes even very good believers (NOTE: In Proverbs 24: verse 9a KJV, it says that "**the thought of foolishness is sin**".) Anyone who wants his prayers answered needs to be forgiven by the Father. There is only one way to start this process. Every prayer should be under the banner of forgiveness. This is done by asking the Father to forgive you of all of the sins that you have committed since the last time you asked for forgiveness. Tell Him you are sorry that you sinned. If you truly meant this prayer, this re-establishes your fellowship with Him. Seeking forgiveness is a lot more than just saying: "Please forgive me of my sins. Amen!" True repentance requires one to be truly sorry and convicted of committing sins. If you are not aware of the sins that you

have committed, spend some time thinking about it. Ask the Father to remind you of sins that you have committed and sins that are ongoing problems.

It is the exclusive function of the Holy Spirit to convict people of their sins (John 16:7-8). Some self-called well-meaning people take this on as their special mission in life. Anyone can be used by God's Holy Spirit but no earthly being has that specific assignment. There is a difference between warning and convicting, read Ezekiel 3:18-19KJV.

> **"When I say unto the wicked, Thou shalt surely die; and thou givest him not warning, nor speakest to warn the wicked from his way, to save his life: the same wicked man shall die in his iniquity: but his blood will I require at thine hand. Yet if thou warn the wicked, and he turn not from his wickedness, nor from his wicked way, he shall die in his iniquity; but thou hast delivered thy sole."**

Ask the Spirit to do His work in your life. Give Him free rein to do as He wishes. He only does the will of the Father. Until you establish or reestablish fellowship with the Master, you are wasting your time trying to pray about other needs and concerns. Many Scriptures relate to this.

a.  I John 1:9 **"If we confess our sins, he is faithful and just to forgive us our sins and to cleanse us from all unrighteousness."**

b.  Psalm 139:23-24 KJV **"Search me, O God, and know my heart: try me, and know my thoughts: And see if there be any wicked way in me, and lead me in the way everlasting."**

c.  Psalms 103:11-12 **"For as high as the heavens are above the earth, so great is his steadfast love toward those who fear him; as far as the east is from the west, so far does he remove our transgressions from us."**

d.  Isaiah 43:25KJV **"I, even I, am he that blotteth out thy transgressions for my own sake, and I will not remember thy sins."**

e.  Ephesians 1:7-8 **"In him we have redemption through his blood, the forgiveness of our trespasses, according to the riches of his grace, which he lavished upon us, in all wisdom and insight making known to us the mystery of his will, according to his purpose, which he set forth in Christ"**

2.  Seeking the LORD – No person on earth is in perfect unity with the Good LORD. It is the individual's responsibility to keep moving closer to Him. He is not that far away. Search the Scriptures. Determine as best you can what God's will is for you. Then strive to do it. If you sense that you need His help, then you are on the right track. When you lack knowledge, ask!

> **"Call to me and I will answer you,**
> **and will tell you great and hidden**
> **things that you have not known."**

Jeremiah 33:3

a.  Jeremiah 29:11-14a **"For I know the plans I have for you, declares the LORD, plans for wholeness and not for evil, to give you a future and a hope. Then you will call upon me and come and pray to me, and I will hear you. You will seek me and find me. When** you seek me with <u>all your heart</u>, I will be found by you, declares the LORD, ..."

b. Amos 5:4 **"For thus says the LORD to the house of Israel: "Seek me and live;"**

c. Psalm 105:3-5 **"Glory is in his holy name; let the hearts of those who seek the LORD rejoice! Seek the LORD and his strength; seek his presence continually! remember the wondrous works that he has done, his miracles, and the judgments he uttered,"**

3. Thanksgiving - Expressions of thanksgiving and praise – When I receive something from another person I try to show them appreciation for the gift. It is more sincere than just saying "thank you" and sending them a kind note. On the other hand, when I choose to give something to another person I want to feel that the gift will be beneficial to them. This is confirmed when they show appreciation. Every believer has many things for which he should be very thankful. The sad truth is that most believers take their blessings for granted. Some may only give token thanks for a few of the extra special big blessings in their life. This is a problem. Every good thing that is in a person's life is worthy of thanksgiving. Everyone should also give thanks for the bad things that are not part of their lives. There are many earned and unearned conditions and occurrences that could have happened or could have been easily attached to any of us. The Good LORD has shielded us from many spiritual diversions; we should be very grateful for His ever-present watchfulness and care.

Most if not all believers need to ask the Father for forgiveness and for being un-appreciative for the many good things that He has already provided for them. This should be followed up with a sincere "Thank You" to the good LORD, who generously gives each of us much more than we could ever deserve. Meditate on the many good things that He has already done. .... One should always live his life in a thankful manner! Should you have any questions about this, you need to make it a serious matter of prayer.

Perhaps you have been spared from a harsh correction because you sincerely repented and changed your behavior. Think about this before you say the words "thank you", think about what you are thankful for. If you are truly thankful, then thank Him! If you are just repeating some prayer words, He knows that too. The Bible speaks directly on the matter of thanksgiving.

a.  Psalm 100:1-5KJV **"Make a joyful noise unto the LORD, all ye lands. Serve the LORD with gladness: come before his presence with singing. Know ye that the LORD he is God: it is he that hath made us, and not we ourselves; we are his people, and the sheep of his pasture. Enter into his gates with thanksgiving, and into his courts with praise: be thankful unto him, and bless his name. For the LORD is good; his mercy is everlasting; and his truth endureth to all generations."**

b.  Psalm 52:8-9KJV **"But I am like a green olive tree in the house of God: I trust in the mercy of God forever and ever. I will praise thee for ever, because thou hast done it: and I will wait on thy name; for it is good before thy saints."**

c.  I Chronicles 29:13 **"And now we thank you, our God, and praise your glorious name."**

d. Psalm 107:1-2KJV **"Oh give thanks unto the LORD, for he is good, for his mercy endureth forever. Let the redeemed of the LORD say so, whom he hath redeemed from the hand of the enemy;"**

e. Psalm 75:1 **"We give thanks to you, O God; we give thanks, for your name is near. We recount your wondrous deeds."**

4. Praise is an excellent way of acknowledging who the Good LORD is to us.

a. Psalm 113:1-4 - When a person truly senses the Good LORD in his life, He will almost automatically began praising Him. When you are not choosing to praise Him, you need to make some serious changes. **"Praise the LORD! Praise, O servants of the LORD, praise the name of the LORD! Blessed be the name of the LORD from this time forth and forevermore! From the rising of the sun to its setting, the name of the LORD is to be praised! The LORD is high above all nations, and his glory above the heavens!"**

b. Psalm 117 1-2KJV **"O Praise the LORD, all ye nations: praise him, all ye people. For his merciful kindness is great toward us: and the truth of the LORD endureth for ever. Praise ye the LORD."**

c. I Corinthians 15:56-57 **"The sting of death is sin, and the power of sin is the law. But thanks be to God, who gives us the victory through our LORD Jesus Christ."**

5. Request that God's will is accomplished - Perhaps, this is the second most important prayer that a believer can utter.

The first being the prayer asking God to forgive him of his sins. A close relative of this is the act of accepting God's will then making His will the sole aim of your life. The truth be known, many times even good believers sometimes disagree with the Father. Too many may think that His will should be more "me" centered. Some may believe that they rate a more important assignment. They may tend to just keep on nagging the Father for a "higher status". Shame on us. Being happy and content with His will is the key to much greater happiness! He assigns the task and His blessings in His own special way. It is counted as wisdom on our part when we joyfully accept His will. Christians are often referred to as followers of Christ. He leads. We follow!

a. Psalms 143:10KJV **"Teach me to do thy will; for thou art my God: thy Spirit is good; lead me into the land of uprightness!"**

b. Matthew 12:50 **"For whoever does the will of my Father in heaven is my brother and sister and mother."**

c. Luke 11:2KJV **"And he said unto them, When ye pray, say, Our Father which art in heaven, Hallowed be thy name. Thy kingdom come. Thy will be done, as in heaven, so in earth."**

6. Intercession for others – When you don't have concern for others, then there is a vacuum in your spiritual life. How can you expect others to care about you when you don't exhibit concern for them?

a. Matthew 8:5b-7 **"When he entered Capernaum, a centurion came forward to him, appealing to him,**

"LORD, my servant is lying paralyzed at home, suffering terribly." And he said unto him, I will come and heal him."

b.  Luke 4:38-39 **"And he arose and left the synagogue and entered Simon's house. Now Simon's mother-in-law was ill with a high fever, and they appealed to him on her behalf. And he stood over her and rebuked the fever, and it left her, and immediately she rose and began to serve them."**

c.  John 4:46-47 **"So he came again to Cana in Galilee, where he had made the water wine. And at Capernaum there was an official whose son was ill. When this man heard that Jesus had come from Judea to Galilee, he went to him and asked him to come down and heal his son, for he was at the point of death."**

7.  Request for meeting our perceived needs: NOTE there is a big difference between what we truly need and what we want. Wanting something a lot does not make it a need!

a.  Psalm 17:6 **"I call upon you, for you will answer me, O God; incline your ear to me; hear my words."**

b.  Psalm 54:2 **"O God, hear my prayer; give ear to the words of my mouth."**

c.  Psalm 55:1-2 **"Give ear to my prayers, O God, and hide not yourself from my plea for mercy! Attend to me, and answer me; I am restless in my complaint and I moan,"**

d. Psalm 102:1-2 **"Hear my prayer, O LORD; let my cry come to you! Do not hide your face from me in the day of my distress! Incline your ear to me; answer me speedily in the day when I call!"**

8. Anything that the Holy Spirit puts on your heart.

These are some of the basic categories. They could be further divided into subcategories. The list of valid prayer possibilities is very long.

Ask yourself, "Has God's Spirit brought to mind something that I should avoid and temptations that I fall easily into?" Are there things I should do differently? What does the Father expect me to do toward squelching some of my more frequent sins?" NOTE 2: He does the work but it is necessary for us to make an honest decision by trusting and obeying Him!

> **"Likewise the Spirit helps us in our weakness. For we do not know what to pray For as we ought, but the Spirit himself intercedes for us with groanings too deep for words. And he who searches hearts knows what is the mind of the Sprit, because the Spirit intercedes for the saints according to the will of God."**
>
> Romans 8:26-27

> **"Until now you have asked nothing in my name. Ask, and you will receive, that your joy may be full."**
>
> John 16:24

"Is anyone among you suffering? Let him pray. Is anyone among you cheerful? Let him sing praise. Is anyone among you sick? Let him call for the elders of the church and let them pray over him, anointing him with oil in the name of the LORD. And the prayer of faith will save the one who is sick, and the LORD will raise him up. And if he has committed sins, he will be forgiven."

James 5:13-16

NOTE: You should pray whenever and for whatever the Holy Spirit places on your heart. Perhaps there have been more prayers offered for healing that any other prayer topic. For ourselves and for others! This topic requires a separate chapter. If not an entire book.

# CHAPTER 4

# HEALING PRAYERS FOR YOURSELF AND OTHERS

I HAVE NEVER BEEN ASKED BY a sick person to not pray for them. Every sick person I have met wants to get better. In the Bible there are many verses that clearly promise healing. Many people pray for healing based on them. A few people are healed instantly. Others are healed over time. Some are healed in death. Occasionally healing prayers appear to go unanswered. What is wrong? Praying for the sick entails much more than just quoting a "healing verse" and pressuring the good LORD do what He has already said He would do!

First of all, each of us needs to get his spiritual condition in alignment with the Father. It is a very rare person that doesn't need some adjustments in their spiritual life. So Far, there has only been only One! Asking for forgiveness is the starting point. After this the believer's most important prayer topics are to request His help in resisting the temptations of Satan and asking that the LORD's will is done! Nothing is more important! But, but, nothing! Secondly, remember that Almighty God is your heavenly Father. He loves each of us very much. He wants the very best for each of us. It is His sincere highest priority for each one of us to be HOLY! He wants us to be like Jesus.

**NB** (nota bene is Latin for note well) Scripture verses are interconnected. Some people correctly refer to the Bible as the Living Word. This is accurate. The Holy Scriptures are organic. They are complex and its verses and their meanings are very interrelated. Most if not all Bible verses relate to and are interwoven with many other verses. Very few verses, if any, can stand 100% alone and convey a complete thought. For example, one of my favorite healing verses is Isaiah 53:5 KJV:

> **"But he was wounded for our transgressions, he was bruised for our iniquities: the chastisement of our peace was upon him; and with his stripes we are healed."**

This verse contains the hopes and the desires of very many believers. If you don't think that you are sick then you don't really know very much about your own body. We are all defective in one way or another. This verse would not be in the Bible if the good LORD hadn't put it there! Let us look closer at it. It was written in about 760 B.C. It is a prophetic promise that Christ would suffer and die and that by means of His suffering He would enable believers to be healed. We are living in the 21$^{st}$ century roughly 2800 years later. NOTE 1: In order for anyone to be healed he must first be sick! Scripture does not indicate how long a person needs to be sick before the good LORD heals him. (This time period could possibly be related to their spiritual condition or circumstances.)

Now ask yourself another question. Has God healed anyone before this verse was written? One example occurred in approximately 894 B.C.

> **"So he went down and dipped himself seven times in the Jordan, according to the word of the man of God, and his flesh was restored like the flesh of a little child, and he was clean."**

> II Kings 5:14

What were the circumstances around this healing? Why was he healed? To bring glory and honor to the Father. Naaman (a non-believer at the time) obeyed God's prophet. He acted in faith. He didn't have very much faith but he acted on the faith that he did have. Read the entire story in (chapter 5 in II Kings). It is an interesting story. Okay, so the story is interesting, but how does this apply to me? Naaman did what the LORD told him to do. He acted on the very small amount of faith that he had. He believed God's prophet and he was healed!

Most people overlook the importance of the little servant girl, even though she was a slave to Naaman, she demonstrated a believer's love for her master. Her act of kindness should put many of us to shame. How often do you pray for the benefit of your boss?

While this is an example of one person's healing it also contains some elements that apply to all of God's promises. Faith and obedience. If the truth be known, each of us has faith and obedience deficiencies. Who are we that we should expect the Almighty to do anything instantly for us just because we requested it? Ask yourself another question, "Did my earthly father give me everything I wanted as soon as I asked him for it?" Our Heavenly Father is much wiser. All believers are God's children. He is our heavenly Father! Should He expect anything less than faith and obedience from each one of His children? ....

A person who is a believer can promise and do all kinds of wonderful things that he believes are in God's will and still be sick. It is not our deeds that make us holy. It is the condition of our heart that matters. When a person's heart is holy, being physically healed becomes a secondary concern. A holy person will be eager to follow Gods Spirit and strive to do His will. And while doing His will he will be looking forward toward the next opportunity on God's things for him to do list.

There is a very good reason why the good LORD allows some of us to be sick. He wants to use our sickness to help us spread the word about Him (John 9:1-7). Are you honoring the LORD with your sickness? What more could you want? It is not that believers have to have a stiff upper lip and stare granite faced into adversity. No! No! When we are sick and have surrendered to His will. Others will see Jesus in us. This is one way the gospel is spread in our cold and cruel world. One might also wonder, "If I project Jesus to the world while being healthy would it be necessary to get sick?" Remember, all life on earth is temporary, each of us is just passing through.

There is another good reason for some to be sick. It is to protect them so that they don't do something harmful to their spirit that would prevent or strongly hinder them from doing God's will.

Looking on a more optimistic side of sickness, suppose the Good LORD does decide to heal us. O happy day! I would suggest that the appropriate way of demonstrating our gratitude would be to daily reflect God's love to everyone that we meet. In some cases, and for some people this is much more difficult that it sounds. The Good LORD knows our self-imposed limitations and He is not going to ask us to do anything that we can't do. With the help of the Holy Spirit anything in His will is possible. With His help, we can also bear any burden that He allows.

An often-asked question is, when is the Good LORD going to heal me? The answer is both simple and complex. He is going to deliver the healing that he promised when the time and circumstances are right. He is going to use the method of addressing our sickness that is best suited for the advancement of His kingdom.

The healing is in his hands. But sometimes the timing is related to our response to His Holy Spirit. If His Spirit were to urge us to go to the Jordan River and dip ourselves in it seven times and we choose not to, then, our lack of healing would be on us. He wants us to be thankful for our healing and to use it to tell others about Jesus. If we are blaming the Almighty for our sickness, then, our lack of healing is our own fault. There are many things we can and should do to get into the right spiritual condition to promote and allow our healing. The chief among these is being humble and completely submissive to the Holy Spirit. The first step in doing this is to ask the Father to forgive us of our sins. As long as a person is harboring even a tiny sin in his heart and choosing his will over the Father's will, no one can reasonably expect the good LORD to heal or to otherwise help him!

Sometimes healing is delayed because of the beliefs and actions of others. Perhaps a spiritually shy person is being led to come and pray boldly for your healing. Perhaps the Good LORD is wanting your healing to help build their faith. We will never know, at least down here what all of His reasons are; but, His Spirit will be urging everyone concerned to do their part in His will.

**NB: All of us eventually die!**

**"And just as it is appointed for man to die once, and after that comes judgement,"**

Hebrews 9:27

This will happen when it becomes God will for us to die. If there is an exception to this time, it would be when we choose to do something very depraved to yourself that is outside of his will. He has given us a free will. We should be constantly aware that along with free will there are always the bad consequences of wrongfully exercising it.

The Bible has clear-cut instructions for a believer, if he desires healing.

**"Is anyone among you sick? Let him call for the elders of the church, and let them pray over him, anointing him with oil in the name of the LORD. And the prayer of faith will save the one who is sick, and the LORD will raise him up. And if he has committed sins, he will be forgiven. Therefore confess your sins to one another and pray for one another, that you may be healed. The prayer of a righteous person has great power as it is working."**

James 5:14-16

Scripture is clear, if you are sick <u>be obedient</u>, **call the elders to pray and anoint you with oil, confess your sins, pray for each**

**other.** If you expect the good LORD to heal you, you are on the right track. **BUT** He also expects you to be obedient. He expects you to confess your sins. He expects you to exercise faith. On the other hand, if you choose to disregard the Scriptures you are making a very bad decision. Believers always have choices! In every decision there are consequences!

# CHAPTER 5

# THE SCOPE OF OUR PRAYERS

Should a believer pray all-encompassing prayers or should a believer include with his prayers specific list of needs and concerns. By all-encompassing I mean prayers that cover everything. For example: "Dear God please bless all of the missionaries all over the world." Or "please help all of the sick people get well." These prayers at best are more suitable for young children who are just learning to pray. Remember, there are non-Christian faiths who have recruiters that they call missionaries. Do you really want the LORD to bless their activities? Well, how about sick people? Suppose it is God's time for someone to die. Everyone eventually dies. That is how God configured life. Do you want to be praying against God's will?

I believe that a better targeted prayer can be more appropriate. Believers should get to know at least a few missionaries by name. When they discuss their missionary activities you should ask questions. If you sincerely want to help them, you will quickly discover their needs. You might be led in some unique way to help them. You might hold the answer to one of their prayers and you might be personally empowered to do something special in God's will that will help spread the gospel.

When someone you know is sick you should pray for them. Your overall prayer should be for God's will to be done. Your detailed prayers could be for their doctors to be given wisdom in treating them. Perhaps in regard to their sickness you hear about a specific problem or special need. It could be temperature, breathing, or blood pressure, whatever is their most urgent concern. An excellent prayer is to ask the Father to take care of that condition. Commit this need to the Father. Ask for His will to be done. Normally, when one problem is cared for another condition becomes the next important issue. Pray for their needs as you become aware of them.

Pray for them exactly the way you would want someone to pray for you, if you were in their condition. You can ask the Father for anything, but make sure that you make it clear that you want His will to override your personal desires. When you sincerely pray for His will to be done, that prayer always gets answered! Hold this thought in mind: The Good LORD loves each one of us very much. He has plans for each of us to do many things in His will. NOTE 1: His will is not what our old sinful nature would want it to be. NOTE 2: As you notice that more and more of your prayers are answered the more spiritual you will become. Being spiritual minded is a first cousin to holiness.

Part of the scope of your prayers includes who you should pray for. First you should pray for yourself. If you are not right with the Almighty and spiritually fit for His service, then how much help will you be able to give to others? Secondly, you should pray for your family. Your influence in spiritual matters will be lacking, if your family obviously needs spiritual help. Next, I would suggest that you pray for your church especially if you are aware of any spiritual needs. After this would come your neighbors and the people that you come in contact with regularly. I put them after your family and church. If they don't sense the overshadowing of the Holy Spirit in your life, then all they will probably think that you are an echo chamber and that you only repeat a bunch of empty words.

As a believer you have a spiritual obligation to pray for everyone who asked you to pray for them. Yes, even those on a news program where someone being interviewed desperately requests prayer. Most importantly, you should pray for whatever and whomever the Holy Spirit prompts you to. Don't get tangled up in asking yourself why the Creator of the universe wants you to pray, just be obedient. Always pray as the Holy Spirit leads. If He wants you to know more details or why He wants you to pray, He will have no difficulty communicating that to you.

# CHAPTER 6

# WHERE SHOULD WE PRAY

"And when you pray, you must not be like the hypocrites. For they love to stand and pray in the synagogues and at the street corners, that they may be seen by others. Truly, I say to you, they have received their reward. But when you pray, go into your room and shut the door and pray to your Father who is in secret. And your Father who sees in secret will reward you."

Matthew 6:5-6

"...for mine house shall be called an house of prayer for all people."

Isaiah 56:7bKJV

BELIEVERS CAN PRAY ANYWHERE, BUT there are some places they shouldn't be. And being there can place them under the weighty influence of Satan. If you are in one of these places, you may need desperate prayers in order to escape.

For some people there is an automatic answer to the where to pray question, "church". For others the automatic answer is wherever you happen to be. A better question could be: What difference does it make where you pray? The answer is complex because there are many different situations and many different types of prayer.

1.  You should pray wherever and whenever God's Holy Spirit moves you to pray. If He is not leading you, then who is?

2. There are event-oriented prayers: You pray where you are when the event happens.

   a. When you sense that you need guidance.
   b. When you experience fear.
   c. When you are in need.
   d. When others need God's help.
   e. When there are special events and you are asked to pray as part of the program. NOTE 1: If you are not allowed to pray a fully Christian prayer in Jesus's name you should consider declining. NOTE 2: you can also pray a legitimate prayer without using the exact words "in Jesus's name". You can address your prayers to: the Father, the LORD, the Almighty, the God of Abraham, Isaac, and Jacob, etc. <u>Exercise wisdom</u>!

3. Your personal daily prayers are normally prayed at the same special place and at an appointed time. These are your in-depth prayers that cover the full range of all your prayer concerns. This prayer will normally be the longest prayer you pray that day. The time and place are determined by you and your circumstances. It is best if it is very quiet and private with no distractions. Some people call this their prayer closet. Nevertheless, it is the place that you have chosen for your quality time with the Father.

> **"And rising very early in the morning, while it was still dark, he departed and went out to a desolate place, and there he prayed."**
>
> Mark 1:35b

   a. It should be private.
   b. It should be quiet.

c. It should be illuminated sufficiently for you to read from your Bible.
d. There should be no distractions.
e. If possible, this place should be used only for prayer.
f. It should be where and whenever the LORD HAS LED YOU to pray.

4. If at all possible, your prayer time should not be sandwiched between two fixed time priorities. When you do this it leaves you with an exact time allotment for prayer which can, by itself, become a distraction. Do you need to set a timer or alarm clock? Do you continually need to glance at a clock to make sure you haven't "over prayed"? These are prayer distractions. For this reason, some have chosen bedtime as their major prayer time. NOTE 3: There are no Scriptures that limit your special prayer times to just once a day. You can have as many special prayer times as you are led to have. More is better.

5. Things that promote distractions during a person's time with the Father should be eliminated. When they can't be eliminated they should at least be minimized as much as reasonable. Prayer time is your special time with the Master. You will have an unproductive prayer life, if while you are praying, you are distracted by thoughts of some other activity. For example: If you have a major prayer time just before an important ball game. Your prayers will be distracted. When you pray there should be no interferences, in your mind or in your environment. Ask yourself what is the most imperative thing to you? If you have any hesitation about putting the good LORD first, then you have serious spiritual problems!

Sometimes I will get an important idea or the solution to a problem that I have been working on just before I pray or even during a prayer. I will jot it down quickly so that I am not further distracted by it while I am praying. There is always something that can distract you. Minimize distractions. You should ask the Father to help you to keep focused on listening to and obeying His Spirit!

# CHAPTER 7

# PRAYER POSTURES

"And Moses quickly <u>bowed his head</u>
toward the earth and worshiped."

Exodus 34:8

"And he said, "No; but I am the
commander of the army of the LORD.
Now I have come," And Joshua <u>fell on his face</u>
to the earth and worshiped and said to him,
"What does my lord say to his servant?"

Joshua 5:14

"Now as Solomon finished offering all this
prayer and plea to the LORD, he arose from
before the altar of the LORD, where he had
<u>knelt with hands outstretched toward heaven.</u>"

I Kings 8:54

And going a little farther <u>he fell on his
face</u> and prayed, saying, "My Father, if
it be possible, let this cup pass from me;
nevertheless, not as I will, but as you will."

Matthew 26:39

THERE ARE MANY PRAYER POSTURES mentioned in Scriptures. All of them are on the approved list. If you are led to pray in a specific posture, use it. If you are not led, you might try each one. Don't let what you think is the result of your prayers over influence you. Leave the influencing part of your prayer to the Holy Spirit. If He leads you to use a posture, use it. You can pray in any physical position. If the Holy Spirit leads you to kneel for prayer, remember that prayer is a spiritual communication. The most important posture is the one that your spirit is in when you are praying. If you are led by the Holy Spirit to have a particular prayer posture in public prayer, don't allow Satan to embarrass you into not using it.

The believer's attitude should always be humble, meek, trusting, patient, thankful, respectful, and most of all he should be wanting the Father's will to be done. There is nothing more important in heaven or on earth than God's will. NOTE 1: If you are in a spirit of rebellion because you suspect you know God's will and don't want to do it, then you are in serious trouble. The Father is very good at correcting rebellion. People bring the fruits of rebellion on themselves.

Prayer postures should not express pride. Don't let your prayers become part of a show. They are not for the purpose of impressing anyone. Prayer is a very humble activity. Ask yourself: Why are there so many Scriptural examples of outstanding believers assuming a prayer posture? What did they know that we have possibly overlooked? Was it a cultural element for them or was it spiritual?

NOTE 2: Prayer postures are normally for special prayers. Your anytime anywhere prayers are also important. They occur when and wherever the Holy Spirit prompts you to pray. Normally, these are one topic prayers. For Example: you are driving down the freeway and suddenly you are prompted to pray for someone you went to high school with 30 years ago. You have no idea about what challenges they are going through right now. You can pray for the Holy Spirit to comfort and guide them and that His will, will be done. You should keep praying for them as long as God's Spirit is prompting you. Don't worry about what you are going to pray about. God's Spirit will supply the words you need. Follow His leading.

The posture of your heart is the most important one. It is best to assume an honest humble posture. This is the posture that is most vital. Don't think that by choosing a good physical posture that the Good LORD will tend to see more things your way. When you bow down you are still facing God. He is everywhere. He is not impressed by our earthly theatrical ability. Trickery and scheming will only result in negative consequences. Always be humble and honest with the Good LORD.

# CHAPTER 8

# PRAYER INTENSITY

How emotionally driven are your prayers? How deep are your heart felt needs? How do you gauge a prayer's emotional intensity? I would suggest two extreme points on the emotional curve. At the bottom of the curve is a "Thank you prayer for the food that you are about to eat." spoken by an over-weight person who is well supplied with good food. The other being a desperate person swept to tears by the intensity of his need in a traumatic life and death, heaven matter. Between them is everything else. An obvious question that one should ask is: What difference does our emotional intensity make to the Father? Personally, I have had prayers answered at just about every intensity level I have experienced. I have also had prayers of just about every intensity seemingly unanswered. I suspect that the Father doesn't get excited when we pump up our emotional state. A true believer prays naturally and honestly expresses his needs to the Father. I believe that a favorable response is more likely for the honest and humble believer. NOTE 1: His response may not be the one we were wanting. Nevertheless, we should always honor and accept His answers or His delay in answering. A delay is often a part of His response.

On the other hand, if the needs that we are praying for are not important to us, then why should the Father pay any attention to them? Some people are more emotionally driven and others appear to be more stoic. When you pray be honest in your attitude. Any effort to hype yourself up in the hope that the good LORD will pay more attention to you is worse than just wasting energy, it is being dishonest with the Father. He may choose to put your prayers on hold until you demonstrate a more mature attitude.

If, however your emotional expressions in your prayer are honest and not part of a scam, then don't worry. The good LORD knows the difference.

For those of us who tend to be more stoic, we need to loosen up and just be emotionally honest with the Master. If you really believe that He loves and understands you, then an honest expression of your needs is appropriate.

Being honest applies to both private and public prayers. Even when you are praying a desperate prayer for someone in great need, you owe it to them to keep the expression and content of your prayer honest. You don't want any dishonesty factors to interfere with someone getting his prayer needs met.

# CHAPTER 9

# REPETITIVE PRAYERS – IS ONCE ENOUGH?

"Be not rash with your mouth, nor let
your heart be hasty to utter a word before
God, for God is in heaven and you are on
earth. Therefore let your words be few.
For a dream comes with much business,
and a fool's voice with many words."

Ecclesiastes 5:2-3

"And when you pray, do not heap up empty
phrases as the Gentiles do, for they think
that they will be heard for their many words.
Do not be like them, for your Father knows
what you need before you ask him."

Matthew 6:7-8

"Woe unto you, scribes and Pharisees,
hypocrites! For ye devour widows' houses,
and for a pretense make long prayer: therefore
ye shall receive the greater damnation."

Matthew 23:14 KJV

THE TOPIC OF REPETITIVE PRAYERS raises some interesting questions. The easy answer is to pray for something or someone as long and as often as the Holy Spirit puts the need to pray in your heart. On the other hand, some people may think that they can wear down the LORD by their persistence. This will not work in your favor! Other times the LORD may be testing your resolve. Ask yourself these questions:

1. If the Good LORD were to give me the answer that I am now wanting, how would it serve His purposes?
2. Do you really want what you are asking for?
3. Why would it be God's will for you to have the answer that you are seeking?
4. Could the thing that you want be outside of His will?
5. Is He wanting you to wait for something else?
6. Could the delay be because someone else is not willing to do some critical element in His will?
7. Is the LORD helping you to develop the virtue of patience?

On the other hand, there is the parable found in Luke chapter 18 that Jesus told regarding persistent prayer. These verses compare prayer to the persistent pleas of a widow who kept on appealing to an earthly judge for help. The earthly judge eventually was worn down and decided to act not because of the rightness of her request but because she kept on calling on him for justice.

Are the Scriptures in conflict? No! Please explain: The good LORD may be testing you. Do you really want the help that you just prayed for? The LORD wants us to see the positive effect of our prayers because each clearly answered prayer makes our faith stronger. Faith is very important to Him.

> **"And without faith it is impossible to please him, for whoever would draw near to God must believe that he exists and that he rewards those who seek him."**
>
> Hebrews 11:6

There is both a good and a bad side in the practice of praying until you get the answer you are seeking. The bad side of this is that you may become obsessed in praying for something that is outside of God's will. NOTE 1: There are some very good things that will honor Christ that are not in God's will for you. The good side of perseverance is that you may be drawn closer to the Father. He can also use you as an example of spiritual perseverance so that others may grow by following your example. They could learn that there is merit in trusting the good LORD over a period of time. It is also evidence that your relationship with the LORD is not casual.

The good side: The more you pray about a concern the more you will tend to refine it into a better-defined prayer that is more sharply focused on God's will being done. It is also a testimony to the Father that you are placing your personal desires on hold so that you can focus on finding and doing His will.

On the bad side: Some people, who are praying outside of God's will may believe that by keeping on and keeping on that they can wear down the Father's resistance and that He will eventually give them exactly what they want just because they were stubborn in prayer. CAUTION: Should you persists out of stubbornness; the Good LORD has a wonderful cure for that. Sometimes He gives the persistent person exactly what he has been begging for so that he will vividly see that God's will is much better and that the answer that they thought that they wanted was not what they truly desired or in fact needed. NOTE 2: Think about the neat car that you got that now requires a lot of expensive maintenance.

Continually pray for God's will to be done. This is a prayer that is always answered in God's perfect timing and demonstrates that you trust the good LORD to take the best action when He determines that the time is right.

It all goes back to one of my opening statements. Each believer has two natures. They are at constant war with each other. It is always best to nurture your new nature by purposefully selecting God's will as your uppermost desire and action.

Now ask yourself a few questions. Why did I pray a second prayer? Was it for a specific reason? What is my reason for repeating the same request over and over again? Am I trying to wear down the good LORD? Or am I demonstrating my reliance in Him? Why is this request so important? Has the LORD already answered my prayer? Then why haven't I accepted His answer? Am I holding out for something that pleases me more? Where is the encouragement for repeating this request coming from? There are only two possible sources. It is either the Holy Spirit or it could be Satan working with your fallen nature to distract you from doing or being in God's will. If you can identify who is influencing you, the reason for repeating your request will become much clearer. Use the brain that the good LORD gave you. Is it His will for you to pray about this concern? Which Scripture verses do you base this on?

NOTE 3: Believers at their best can only ask. The Good LORD always chooses what He is going to do. There is only one known exception in Scripture.

In Joshua 10 vs.12-14 it says,

> **"At that time Joshua spoke to the LORD
> in the day when the LORD gave the
> Amorites over to the sons of Israel,
> and he said in the sight of Israel,
> and he said in the sight of Israel,
> "Sun, stand still at Gibeon, and moon,
> in the Valley of Aijalon." And
> the sun stood still and the moon
> stopped, until the nation took
> vengeance on their enemies. Is this
> not written in the Book of Jashar?
> The sun stopped in the midst of heaven
> and did not hurry to set for
> about a whole day. There has been no
> day like it before or since, when
> the LORD obeyed the voice of a man,
> for the LORD fought for Israel."**

When you pray remember that the LORD doesn't have to do anything that you request. It is always His choice in everything that He does. Pray humbly!

When a person is truly hurting the follow up prayers are mostly for reassurance and provide additional fellowship time with the Father. This is a good thing in itself. Fellowship with the Father is one of the reasons we were created. Cherish your personal time with Him.

## CHAPTER 10

# WHEN DOES THE FATHER CHOOSE TO ANSWER PRAYERS?

THERE IS AN EASY ANSWER for this question, when it suits Him. He knows when we are ready to obey Him. He knows when others are ready to cooperate with His actions. It is most important to simply trust Him. The answers to some prayers are set into motion before we ask (Isaiah 65:24). Other prayers are answered as we pray. Some are answered at a future time of the Father's choosing. It sometimes seems as if there are an excessive number of prayers that are unanswerable because they never arrive in the throne room. Could it be that God's Spirit, acting out of kindness to us, has placed them in a discarded prayer receptacle? NOTE 1: Answerable prayers are based on an active faith grounded in God's Word.

Closely related to this is another and perhaps more important question. When and how do we realize that He has answered a prayer? Many prayers are answered and we never realize it because we haven't reached out in faith sufficiently to latch on to His answer. When we weren't looking for anything to happen because we really didn't expecting anything to happen it is a definite faith deficiency. So sad! The reasons for this vary. Unfortunately, most of the time we just didn't expect an answer to our prayers. A confirmed lack of faith. Or perhaps we got an answer and didn't like it.

Whatever His answer is, our obligation is to embrace it and to thank Him for it. Stop and think about this for a moment. The all-wise all-powerful Creator of the universe, who loves each of us very much, choose to answer our request. He did it for His own reasons. The number one reason for His answer is that He truly loves us. He consistently wants the best for each of us. He wants each one of His children to be holy!

A question for each believer should be, "When we sense that He hasn't answered a prayer could it be that the answer that we wanted would not lead us to be more like Jesus?" We seldom know what a request might eventually accomplish. There are good and bad consequences to almost everything we do. Some requests are obvious even before we ask them. If we were to be honest with ourselves, we would quickly realize that many of our requests would not lead us toward being more like Jesus.

It would be better if these requests were left unasked. Let me explain: Perhaps as a child we were to pray for a new toy. We saw it on TV and thought that it would be fun to play with. So, we ask our heavenly Father for one. If we consider the normal categories of prayer answers as yes, no, and later, we might conclude these possibilities:

> If His answer is yes: It could be that by using the toy that the child he would be drawn him closer to Jesus.

> If His answer is no: It could be that He knows that the toy would cause the child harm.

> If His answer is later: It could be that the act of waiting and depending on Him would strengthen the child's faith.

These are only a few of the many possibilities. Now use your imagination. It is always to your advantage to welcome whatever He decides is the best current answer for you. It's now time for a reality check. Even as a mature believer how many of your request are in fact request for new toys or a nicer life? This being the case we should be brought to our knees in an extended forgiveness prayer. This should be followed up in our next prayers with a more righteous line of thought. When our prayers are more in keeping with righteousness and holiness the number of yeses will increase. What is your spiritual batting average?

Some prayers are always appropriate: Prayers for forgiveness, prayers for salvation, prayers of thanksgiving, prayers of praise, and prayers for God's will to be done. Successful prayers will be saturated with petitions for His will to be done.

When someone asks the Father to do something outside of His will, He may exercise His option to not act on the prayer. For example: In the book of Deuteronomy Moses pleaded with God to allow him to enter the promise land. The LORD responded:

"And the LORD said to me, "**Enough from you; do not speak to me of this matter again.**"

Deuteronomy 3:26b

In II Corinthians Paul prayed to the LORD for healing.

**"Three times I pleaded with the LORD about this, that it should leave me. But he said to me," "<u>My grace is sufficient for you, for my power is made perfect in weakness.</u>""**

II Corinthians 12: 8-9a

On the other hand, when two or more believers are led by His Spirit to agree that something is in God's will; He answers. It is very important to consider the context of Matthew 18:19. NOTE 2: verse 15 it is obvious that verse 19 applies to sins against you and disagreements between two believers. When they confess their sins and agree on a solution that is in God's will, God will support their unity and combined faith. NOTA BENE: Agreeing is not a matter of two or more "believers" ganging up on the good LORD in order for them to get what they want! In these verses the main thyme is Christian unity.

**"Again I say to you, if two of you agree on earth about anything they ask, it will be done for them by my Father in heaven."**

Matthew 18:19

# CHAPTER 11

# PRAYERS THAT ARE ALWAYS ANSWERED

- NOTE 1: More prayers are answered than any of us realize. Few people are so sensitive to the actions of the Holy Spirit that they can confidently identify most of God's activities in their lives. Occasionally, even the dullest of us can clearly discern a special Godly action with certainly. Perhaps, if we made His will a higher priority, we would become more aware of His actions.

- NOTE 2: When His answer is NO! It is an answered prayer!

THERE ARE, HOWEVER, SOME PRAYERS that are always answered in the affirmative! You ask for it and you automatically receive it. But even these prayers you have conditions that must be met. Some might say: "I knew it, there is always a catch". Hold on; it is something that you can control. One of the most important factors is that you must sincerely mean what you are praying. You are not just quoting some prayer phrases or mimicking someone else's prayer. I am convinced that there are at least three sincere heart felt prayers that are always answered, in the affirmative:

1. Dear LORD please forgive me of my sins, save me from the eternal punishment that I deserve, and let me live forever with you in heaven.
2. Dear LORD please forgive me of a specific sin.
3. Dear LORD may your will be done.

Prayer number one is the salvation prayer. It can be phrased in many ways. However, the basic content is the same.

Prayer number two is very similar to prayer number one. This is the prayer a believer prays when he is convicted of sinning by the Holy Spirit and he ask the LORD for His forgiveness. This prayer restores a believer's personal fellowship with the Father.

Prayer number three is the key to taking care of all of the rest of your prayer needs. Keep this thought constantly in mind as you pray. As a believer, God is your heavenly Father and He loves you very much. He desires to do many good things for each of His children. He knows the long-range outcome of each of our request even before they are spoken. By tempering each request with the sincere honest desire that you want His will **to override** your personal wishes, you have prayed an answerable prayer.

> **"And this is the confidence that we have in him, that, if we ask any thing according to his will, he hears us: And if we know that he hears us, whatsoever we ask, we know that we have the requests that we desired of him."**
>
> I John 5:14-15KJV

An example of this is found in the life of Ezra. In (Ezra 7:10) it states that he set his heart to study the Word and to do it. In vs. 18 we see that God moved the king to grant him whatever he needed to do God's will and if any money was left over He could use it to do more of God's will. As a result the king also offered Ezra whatever else he needed to finish the work that God had assigned to him. NOTE 3: There was no reference to the king being a believer. When God's spirit chooses to move anyone to do something; it gets done. He can use anyone that He chooses to accomplish a task. His will is done!

NOTE 4: Because of our fallen nature some things are difficult for us to accept as God's will. Study His Word and pray for wisdom in the matters that bother you. Each one of them holds the potential for spiritual growth. The more you feed and encourage your old sin nature the harder this becomes!

Both God's actions and His will are very complex. The human mind can only comprehend a very small fraction of them. When you have sincerely made a request to the Father that His will is done, the next appropriate prayer is to thank Him for doing whatever He chose to do or not do. Since His will is often different from what we would like it to be, it is good to ask Him to open your eyes so that you can see His hand at work and the ability to better discern and appreciate His will so that you can follow Him more confidently.

When you have a problem accepting His answer, you have a spiritual problem that requires attention. Ask Him to help you embrace His will. Ask Him to lead you to a Scripture verse that sheds additional light on what His will is. Keep in mind that Satan is trying for all he is worth to weaken your faith and your spiritual resolve to follow the Master. Be on guard. He is constantly fighting against God's will being done! Ask yourself, "Whose side are your actions and attitude benefiting"?

The advantages of this are clear. The more you see that the good LORD is acting in response to your prayers the more your faith will grow. The more your faith grows the closer you will be to the Master. The closer you are to the Master the more you will be praying to Him. Instead of being in a downward vicious cycle you will be in a glorious upward spiral. Realizing that your prayers are consistently answered is a wonderful faith building experience.

> **"But without faith it is impossible to please Him: for he that cometh to God must believe that he is, and that he is a rewarder of them that diligently seek him."**
>
> Hebrews 11:6 KJV

# CHAPTER 12

# HINDRANCES TO PRAYER

## "If I regard iniquity in my heart, the LORD will not hear me:"

Psalms 66:18 KJV

**"but your iniquities have made a separation between you and your God, and your sins have hidden his face from you so that he does not hear. For your hands are defiled with blood and your fingers with iniquity; your lips have spoken lies; your tongue mutters wickedness."**

Isaiah 59:2-3

**"For if you forgive others their trespasses, your heavenly Father will also forgive you, but if you do not forgive others their trespasses, neither will your Father forgive your trespasses."**

Matthew 6:14-15

THESE VERSES EXPLAIN SOME OF the main reasons for failures in prayer to make a positive contact with the good LORD. To **regard iniquity in your heart**" means to hold on to your pet sins and to choose not to give them up. Many people try to rationalize or justify a sin. This includes liking a sin so much that you don't ask the Father to forgive you for committing and recommitting it. You cherish it and hold on tightly to it. This is why the majority of people who think that they are believers, are spiritually bankrupt. Their prayers cannot be answered!

"Because I have called, and ye refused; I have stretched out my hand, and no man regarded;"... "Then shall they call upon me, but I will not answer; they shall seek me early, but they shall not find me:"

Proverbs 1:24 & 28 KJV

"Because they hated knowledge and did not choose the fear of the LORD, would have none of my counsel and despised all my reproof, therefore they shall eat the fruit of their way, and have their fill of their own devices."

Proverbs 1:29-31

"If one turns away his ear from hearing the law, even his prayer is an abomination."

Proverbs 28:9

"When you spread out your hands, I will hide my eyes from you; even though you make many prayers, I will not listen; your hands are full of blood.

Isaiah 1:15

"There is no one who calls upon your name, who rouses himself to take hold of you; for you have hidden your face from us, and have made us melt in the hand of our iniquities."

Isaiah 64:7

"As I called, and they would not
hear, so they cried, and I would not
hear, says the LORD of host,"

Zechariah 7:13

"And I will surely hide my face in that day
because of all the evil that they have done,
because they have turned to other gods."

Deuteronomy 31:18

When someone cries out to you and you choose not to pay attention to them the LORD will do the same to you especially if you have been disregarding His written Word.

"For if you forgive others their trespasses, your
heavenly Father will also forgive you, but if you
do not forgive others their trespasses, neither
will your Father forgive your trespasses."

Matthew 6:14-15

"But let him ask in faith, with no doubting,
for the one who doubts is like a wave of the
sea that is driven and tossed by the wind. For
that person must not suppose that he will
receive anything from the LORD; he is a
double-minded man, unstable in all his ways."

James 1:6-7

"You ask and do not receive, because you
ask wrongly, to spend it on your passions."

James 4:3

"When you spread out your hands, I will hide my eyes from you; even though you make many prayers, I will not listen; your hands are full of blood. Wash yourselves; make yourselves clean; remove the evil of your deeds from before my eyes; cease to do evil, learn to do good; seek justice, correct oppression; bring justice to the fatherless and plead the widow's cause."

Isaiah 1:15-17

"Then they will cry out to the LORD, but he will not answer them; he will hid his face from them at that time, because they have made their deeds evil."

Micah 3:4

One of the greatest self-imposed hindrances to victorious prayer is the unexpressed thought that when you pray you don't really expect anything to happen. This is an extreme indication of a faith deficiency. **NOTE: When the LORD says something once it is very important. When He says it many times it is a very, very important truth. ….**

People pray all the time. It is almost like a slot in a program. You ask someone to open a meeting with prayer. Prayer seems to make the event more official. It is often misused as a way of calling a meeting to order because most people are quite when they hear someone pray. Empty prayers do much harm in that they condition people to not expect a response from God. When a person doesn't expect the Good LORD to answer his prayers, his faith takes a nose dive.

"But without faith it is impossible to please him: for he that cometh to God must believe that he is, and that he is a rewarder of them that diligently seek him."

Hebrews 11:6 KJV

Many people also seem to be spiritually hard of hearing. They have conditioned themselves to not put forth any effort to listen to what the good LORD is saying to them. Unless they are actively seeking God's answer they will find it more difficult to recognize His response, if it is presented. To some people prayer is similar to playing the national anthem before a ball game. It is just what people do. To them it has no life changing significance. By disrespecting prayer, they are in effect cutting themselves off from the possibility of supernatural help from the Almighty. This is not to say that Satan isn't doing everything that he can to hinder your prayers. He is not a slacker. He prefers that no one discovers that he is working against your spiritual communications with the Master.

Unless God does exactly what some people request they fail to accept or notice His answer. He knows what we need much better than we do. He also knows what will strengthen our faith and what will weaken us. His gifts are designed to promote His purpose in the believer's life.

**"....seek, and you will find; ..."**

Matthew 7:7b KJV

Husbands have an extra set of responsibilities. If they fail in these their prayers will be hindered!

**"Likewise, ye husbands, dwell with them according to knowledge, giving honor unto the wife, as unto the weaker vessel, and as being heirs together of the grace of life; that your prayers be not hindered."**

I Peter 3:7KJV

Getting back on the right track is not complicated, though it may be more challenging for some. When a person has ignored

God's pleas for a long time it is more stressful for them to repent and the turnaround is much more difficult. His cure is often not what we would like it to be. Sometimes it involves an extreme action by the Father that returns the "Fear of the LORD" to our hearts. When the errant believer decides to return from his backslidden ways, the solution to the unanswered prayer problem is simple. He only needs to sincerely ask the Father for forgiveness and for His help and the spiritual strength to overcome the ongoing temptations of Satan. To do anything less is to invite increased problems.

The Holy Spirit is much better at convicting a believer of ongoing sins than Satan is at getting the believer to resist the pressures of the Holy Spirit and repent and turn from their wicked ways. Any believer can freely choose to have a spiritually improved life. The Father will give you help in response to your prayers. It is always up to you. Sometimes the help he gives is similar to self-discovery stimulated by the Holy Spirit. Here the unrepentant will roll in the slime and mud pits of sin until the stench of sin is just too much for him to bare. At some point the unrepentant will be pressed to make a critical faith decision. How much grief do you need in order to repent and choose to do God's will?

# CHAPTER 13

# HOW OFTEN SHOULD WE PRAY? – PART 1

**"Pray without ceasing,"**

I Thessalonians 5:17 KJV

**"Seek the LORD and his strength;**
**seek his presence continually!**

I Chronicles 16:11

**"Watch ye therefore, and pray always, that**
**ye may be accounted worthy to escape**
**all these things that shall come to pass,**
**and to stand before the Son of Man."**

Luke 21:36 KJV

PRAY ONCE A DAY. (ALWAYS be in prayer.) Your communications with the Father should be never ending! Restated one could say to never hang up or put Him on hold. Keep your communication lines always open to the LORD.

Part of continuous prayer is related to our human prospective. Each of our senses should be constantly aware and supportive of God's hand at work. When we smell a beautiful flower we should breathe words of thanks to the Father for making life more pleasant. When we feel the warm handshake of a friend or the gentile nuzzling of a young puppy we should be reminded that the Good LORD dearly loves each of us. When we see an awesome sunrise, we should feel secure in the fact that the Good LORD is governing the universe. When we hear the chirping in a nest full of young birds, we should express thanks that the Father is constantly providing us with the things that we need.

Our senses bring us much information. It is up to us to choose to look for God's hand at work and to use this awareness as an opportunity to fellowship with the Creator of the universe.

When a person is in a constant prayerful state he will become even more aware of the things that he should be thankful for. The person that is spiritually alert will also notice things and people in his environment that are out of kilter with the Father. This should almost automatically become the basis for additional conversations with the Almighty. These prayers should express a willingness to be active in whatever the good LORD wants you to do. (NOTE 1: By being in a prayerful state the believer will also be more aware that another person is or is not a believer.)

Think about having a direct telephone line to the Master. It is always connected. It is not necessary to redial His number. All you need to do is talk and listen. This connection should never be broken. Sin is a disconnection on your end. Reconnect with a forgiveness prayer immediately!

When we sin God's Holy Spirit will remind us that we need to reestablish communications with the Father. He will encourage us to ask for His forgiveness. A sincere heart felt honest forgiveness prayer is the only way anyone can restore this vital linkage.

# CHAPTER 14

# HOW OFTEN SHOULD
# WE PRAY? - PART 2

NOTE 1: JUST BECAUSE THE last chapter was very short you shouldn't just scan it quickly. Stop and meditate on the Scripture verses. The longer and deeper you meditate on God's Word the better equipped you will be.

Believers should pray every time the Holy Spirit prompts them to pray. Another time to pray is when someone specifically ask for pray. It doesn't matter who they are or even if they are asking for prayer over a radio or TV program. We should pray for their true needs. Trust God's Spirit to guide you as you pray.

Oftentimes, when a person looks you in the eye and ask you to pray for their need you should immediately bow your head and pray out loud for God to help them in the best way that He can. Normally, they will have an overwhelming concern that merits a sincere heartfelt prayer. Follow the leading of God's Spirit. This will be a prayer that the people who have never been prayed for out loud before will long remember. When it is done under the direction of God's spirit it will have a very positive influence on them. It will also have a very good effect on you. You will most likely be led to pray vocally for others. Just as silent prayer has its place, bold oral prayer is very special. A meekly made request normally demonstrates less faith than a heartfelt bold oral request to the Good LORD.

**"And without faith it is impossible
to please Him, …."**

Hebrews 11:6a

There are many ways that people make prayer requests. Even the heathen can make prayer requests. Wait a minute. How can this be? Most heathen don't have a clue about their spiritual needs; they don't know God much less have a desire to pray to Him. Many times, their requests are made in an unusual manner. For example, someone cuts you off in traffic or shakes their fist at you. This could be their way of requesting prayer. Hold on a minute. That is a bit too strange. Let's think about it. Do you honestly think that they need prayer? Do you think that they have anyone else who will pray for them?

There are many people who need prayer. (NOTE 1: Can you name someone who doesn't need prayer?) Many of them are hostel toward those who could help them. Why would anyone choose to pray for someone who expressed anger toward him? The only person who can be expected to pray sincerely for a person like that is a believer who is acting under the leadership of the Holy Spirit. If you haven't prayed for people in this type of situation, then the question for you is: "Why haven't you?"....

Can you give a good reason for not praying for them to get saved? Do you think that they are good believers who are following the Master? Do you think they need prayer? On the other hand, who or what do you think is discouraging you from praying for them? If you can't come up with a good answer to these questions then you, too, are in need of prayer.

As your prayer life improves it will be easier and more normal for someone to ask you to pray for their heartfelt needs. The more you pray the more people you will help spiritually. Increasing your proactive prayer times and the spiritual content of your prayers are a very good set of up-grades.

# CHAPTER 15

# WHEN SHOULD WE PRAY?

**"Pray without ceasing,"**

I Thessalonians 5:17

TAKEN LITERALLY WE SHOULD BE praying all the time. In another sense we should pray every time God's Spirit prompts us to pray. It might be useful to think of prayer in the same way that television sets are made. When you turn on a TV that hasn't been plugged in it will take a longer time to warm up and start working. To overcome this start-up, delay electronic engineers have designed a stand-by circuit. When the TV is plugged in, the stand-by circuit is activated. When it is time to turn the TV on, the stand-by circuit has already warmed up so that the TV doesn't have to wait very long to operate. A believer's prayer life should always be ready to instantly activate from a plugged-in stand-by mode. It is the believer's obligation to be always able and ready to pray to the good LORD on a second's notice. Hence the pray with-out ceasing verse. The same analogy is also true in regard to listening to what the Good LORD has to say to you!

The question is: How does a believer keep in peak spiritual condition where he can instantly be in contact with his Master? It is not as difficult as it might seem. First the believer must keep current in asking the Father to forgive him of his sins. (By now you have noticed that I have written this many times. The reason is very obvious. It is critically important!) Secondly, the believer needs to constantly cultivate his relationship with the Holy Spirit so that he is not doing anything that would distract him from paying attention to the Spirit who leads him to do the will of the Father.

In practice a believer should be consciously praying on and

off all during the entire day. As soon as a prayer need is sensed in his heart, the spiritually alert believer will began praying about it. Granted most of these prayers are abbreviated and concise. They are like "first aid" prayers. They will do until a longer, non-interrupted private prayer time arises.

For most people their dedicated prayer time is either in the mornings or in the evenings. These are the longer prayers and are as detailed as they need to be. They are more complete and heart-felt prayers. This is a critical part of a believer's fellowship time with the Father. Because He loves each of us he takes pleasure in our praying to Him. Perhaps this is why we were created in the first place. If so, when a believer is not praying he is probably in some stage of spiritual rebellion. Hence, the "pray without ceasing" command.

Ask yourself this important diagnostic question. How often, when you are minding your own business and doing some necessary tasks, has the Good LORD brought someone's name to your awareness with the attached thought that you should pray for them? If you regularly pray, based on the prompting of the Holy Spirit, then it is a good indicator that you are spiritually healthy. On the other hand, if you find this a bit strange or a bit too bold and you can't recall many times, if any, when God's Spirit has prompted you to pray for someone out of the blue, then, you most likely have a spiritual problem.

If praying for someone without verbal prompting is a new experience for you and you want some advice, then here it is. As a believer who is seeking to do God's will, you will find that this is a good way for you to begin to participate with the Father in doing His will. First, think of someone that you haven't thought of for some time; a friend from grammar school, a neighbor that you played with as a child. Perhaps, it is someone you used to work with. Don't worry about why He wants you to pray for them, just pray for them.

But what do I pray for? I've got to say something. You can start with an easy prayer. "Dear God, please help _____ to be the man or woman that you want him to be. Please help him to grow spiritually, please help him to be useful to your kingdom and to stand with you in life's challenges. Please help him to be victorious in his spiritual struggles and keep him safe." You may even ask the Father to prompt him to pray for your needs. As you do this you should began to experience more of God's communications in your life.

If after some time has passed, you don't become aware of anything happening, then you might need to have a good sit-down meeting with a spiritually strong believer or a pastor who cares for you. Earthly help is available and it can also be very beneficial. For some spiritual needs it may be good to have an accountability partner. Whether it's a formal meeting or a casual, "How are you doing?" Having someone who truly cares for you and your spiritual condition is important. As they pray for you, you should also be praying for them. This is another benefit of being associated with a congregation of believers wherever you may be.

# CHAPTER 16

# WHAT SHOULD WE NOT PRAY FOR?

**"You ask and do not receive, because you ask wrongly, to spend it on your passions."**

James 4:3

Hey, wait a minute. I thought that we could pray about everything. We can, but there are some things that we shouldn't pray for. One of these is for the spiritual downfall of others. If they are doing something that you know to be wrong, you should pray that God's Holy Spirit would convict them of their sins and that they would repent and surrender to Christ as their LORD and Savior.

Another do not pray item is for the means of satisfying your selfish passions. The word "passions" is used here in the general sense of any kind of immoral aspirations. You shouldn't ask the Good LORD to help you satisfy any sinful desires that your lower nature cultivates. It would be the equivalent prayer of a demented person asking the Father to help them to be able to sin more frequently and in a more enjoyable way. (NOTE 1: Greed is one of these passions! A very big one.)

This seems a bit too ridiculous to even consider. But first, let's take a look at it. Suppose you are driving around on a Sunday afternoon and decide to visit a state park, a nice one with a large lake. Well, there is nothing wrong with that. It can promote tranquility. You look out over the lake and see a lot of attractive active people water skiing. That too is normal. So, what is the big deal? About this time your mind begins to wonder: "I bet if I had a boat like that I would have a lot of attractive friends hanging around me." Next you try to figure out how you could afford such a nice boat. Doing your math, you determine that if you economized all summer that by fall you might be able to afford a small second-hand canoe. Well, that will not work. It would not attract anyone that I would want to be around.

Oh, what can I do? It's about here that your mind goes wacky. Perhaps, if I were to use the boat to pass out tracks on Sunday to people who didn't go to church, maybe the Good LORD would provide me with a nice boat. Then you pray or at least you think you were praying. "Please provide me with a snazzy boat, one that is newer and a bit faster than the one I saw today. Amen". There it is, another prayer that shouldn't be prayed.

Hey, wait a minute, I am not that spiritually dumb. Well let's scale back the boat to something more realistic. It too is not an acceptable prayer topic. Just because a particular lust item is not gigantic doesn't mean that it is any more acceptable to the Father. Perhaps you just want a nice ice cream soda. You know it is off your diet plan, but you think that the Good LORD wants you to be happy and right now a cold soda would do the trick. If you want anything that would work against you being the person that the Good LORD intends you to be, then don't pray for it. The LORD doesn't work against Himself!

Now I ask you to do one more thing. Look at your prayer list and see if there is anything or anyone that the Father would have you add or remove.

When you are praying for something tell the Father what you want. This is basic honesty, you do it because He cares for you. Then, make it clear that you want His will to override your personal desires, in case your petition is for anything that is outside of His will. You can never go wrong by asking for His will to be done! It's more than showing respect. It is a valid demonstration that you trust the Almighty and that you rely on the fact that He loves you very much.

# CHAPTER 17

# DESPERATE PRAYER

From time-to-time unexpected tragedy visits each of us. Everyone eventually gets his turn. Sometimes it is the result of events that some might described as random. We humans seldom accept the fact that our spiritual, mental and physical condition is normally the result of our choices. In many cases desperate circumstances arise out of our own bad decisions. When tragedy strikes one needs very little prompting to pray. It is done almost as a reflexive reaction. When we become aware of imminent doom, we will pray with every bit of spiritual energy that we can muster. The good LORD has no problem getting our full attention!

> **"So we fasted and implored our God for this, and he listened to our entreaty."**
>
> Ezra 8:23

> **"And when they had prayed, the place in which they were gathered together was shaken, and they were all filled with the Holy Spirit and continued to speak the word of God with boldness."**
>
> Acts 4:31

Most desperate prayers are just that. You quickly become keenly aware that the Good LORD's help is the only hope for you in a terrible situation. NOTE 1: Nevertheless, you should always ask for the LORD's will to be done. NOTE 2: Outcomes are always better when you ask the Good LORD to help with lesser problems, even the ones that you think that you can handle by yourself. When events become desperate, you will pray instantly and instinctively. You will probably pray loudly, tearfully and frantically.

Normally, when you pray you begin with confession of your sins, if there is time, you should. You will also be so totally absorbed in the moment that confession is probably not at the top of your prayer agenda. Desperate prayer is one of many reasons why you should keep your forgiveness prayers current. You never know when a sudden unexpected emergency will occur and you will be praying desperately in the few seconds that you may have left. Sometimes a desperate prayer is only one phone call away.

Desperate prayers are just that. An intense life challenging emergency has suddenly dropped on you. The need may be about a loved one thousands of miles away. There is nothing else that you can do. You will pray until you either can't pray any more or until the Good LORD gives you peace. The more prepared you are for that awful occasion the better off you will be.

So how do I get prepared? First you will never know what the occasion might be or what reason you will have for desperate prayer. You will not know when it will be needed. It could happen so quickly that the only prayer that you have time to pray is a "HELP" prayer. It consists of only one word.

# HELP!

Well, Okay. I still need to be prepared. What do I need to do?

1. Keep your sins confessed and forgiveness' prayers current.
2. Memorize as many basic prayer promises as you can.
3. Use the brain that the good LORD gave you and don't venture into bad situations!

4. Try to keep your daily walk in the center of God's will.
5. Make a written list of prayer warriors that you can rely on and that you can contact quickly. Keep the paper list on your person. It could be that you will be unconscious and the LORD might bring a wayfaring stranger to you who will contact them for you.
6. Begin every day with a prayer for God's guidance and protection.
7. End every day with a "thank you" prayer for His help, guidance and protection.

So, what if it happens before I can get ready. It happens and you will do the best that you can do. No one is ever completely ready for a tragedy where desperate prayer is called for, **NO ONE!**

NOTE 3: The Good LORD allows things to happen for His own reasons. Sometimes it is a test, sometimes it is a correction. Most of the time it is for a combination of purposes. It can also be a byproduct of someone else's actions or something that we totally brought on ourselves. When it happens, you will want all the Devine help you can muster so that you can get out from under the terrible event. Often times the help that the LORD provides will be from an unexpected source.

It may also be possible to avoid some of these tragic events by staying in God's Will. Some bad events are unavoidable. Everyone is guaranteed at least one final tragic event. Death! Everyone needs to be ready! ….

> **"Trust in the LORD with all thine
> heart; and lean not unto thine own
> understanding. In all thy ways acknowledge
> him, and he shall direct thy paths."**
>
> Proverbs 3:5-6KJV

Begin every journey or new endeavor the same way. Commit them to the LORD for His safe keeping and for guidance asking that His will is done. It's your life. It will be a lot better if you have the LORD's help and follow His leading. His promises in the Word are a good starting point toward understanding what kinds of help the good LORD has already guaranteed to provide. Scripture does not define the limits to what the LORD will do. He can do fantastic special things when He chooses. It's always up to Him. This is why it is so very important to be continually saturated with His Holy Word and in constant fellowship with the Father.

> **"Confess your faults one to another,**
> **and pray one for another, that ye may**
> **be healed. The effectual fervent prayer**
> **of a righteous man availeth much."**
>
> James 5:16KJV

It is to your advantage to be as righteous as possible all the time. This can only be done with the help and detailed guidance of the Holy Spirit. You will never regret being spiritually prepared! As soon as you have even a hint that there is a bad possibility approaching. You should commit the outcome to the Good LORD! Trust continually in His gracious provisions and protecting hand. Sometimes He will encourage you to make other preparations. Follow His leading. Should He lead you to stay home and not to go somewhere; then that could be His escape plan for you. It all comes back to one central thought. When you trust and obey Him there is no better way!

> **"No temptation has overtaken you that**
> **is not common to man. God is faithful,**
> **and he will not let you be tempted beyond**
> **your ability, but with the temptation**
> **he will also provide the way of escape,**
> **that you may be able to endure it."**
>
> I Corinthians 10:13

NOTE 4: Why wait until a situation gets desperate. Keep your prayer line up to date and in good working order!

NOTE 5: If you have made it a practice to call on the LORD for the smaller needs of life, then when an earth-shattering need arises you will be better able to more competently commit it to the good LORD!

Many people, who practice the martial arts, practice and train for many long hours. They do all this for the very few moments when they might be under physical attack. As a believer we are always under attack. Believers should proportionally study God's Word and prepare ourselves spiritually for the attacks that occur every day.

Another type of desperate prayer involves bad situations that tend to malinger around with possible very bad consequences. In these situations, you will probably have time for long extended prayers. You may be led to fast and pray tearfully. For example, see (Esther 4:16). Here the lives of her nation and herself were in great danger. These prayers tend to be very long and spiritually tiring but they are absolutely necessary. NOTE 6: If you're physical condition is such that you shouldn't do a traditional fast you might try a media fast where you give up newspapers, magazines, television, radio, and the internet and eat and drink humble, less tasteful food. Always follow the leading of the Holy Spirit!

# CHAPTER 18

# DANGEROUS PRAYERS

THERE ARE SOME PRAYERS THAT are very risky to pray. Praying them can place the one who prays them in a dangerous position. (NOTE 1: Praying these prayers may also be very necessary!) I remember hearing a retired missionary pray one of these. He was very concerned about his son. The missionary believed that his son was not a true believer. He prayed that his son would accept Jesus as his Savior. He concluded his prayer by adding "Whatever it takes." He understood exactly what this meant. He was placing his life on the line. He was willing for the Good LORD to take his life or damage his body if that was what it took for his son to become a believer. By the way, his son did get saved and this time the missionary did not have to suffer physically.

Another extreme is the formula prayer. Here the semi-enlightened misuse Scripture by composing a prayer formula. They arrange their prayer words and phrases so that they think that the Almighty will end up **having to do their bidding**. They might even begin one of these prayers by repeating the words, "please forgive me of all of my sins." Saying the correct words without meaning them is worse than valueless. It is delusional. After repeating some forgiveness words, the person with the formula prayer will often jump to a verse that mentions something that he wants. He then believes that by just quoting his series of formula verses that God will automatically have to do whatever he wants done. This is a mirage and is definitely not the same as claiming a Scriptural promise.

Claiming a promise is a spiritual experience that is prompted and empowered by the Holy Spirit. By using very similar words and by not being led by God's Spirit the person using a formula prayer is making a mockery of prayer and Scriptural promises. He probably thinks that he has obligated the good LORD to do whatever he requested. He probably thinks that he has figured out God. Any prayer that is not underscored with the bottom line being that God's will is done, above everything else can be suspect.

**NOTE 2: Be on guard, many of these prayer formulas are so carefully crafted that only the Good LORD** knows whether or not they are a deeply spiritual prayer or a formula prayer. **NOTE 3: DO NOT MAKE JUDGEMENTS REGARDING SOMEONE ELSES PRAYERS!** That is an **exclusive** function of the Holy Spirit. On the other hand, it may be a worthwhile use of your time to think about some of the items that you have prayed about. Ask yourself: Why would the Good LORD choose to help me with this? How would this request advance His kingdom? Is it possible that this request is outside of His will? Is there a Scripture verse that indicates that this could be part of one of God's productions?

Some inappropriate prayers may provoke severe corrections. Tread carefully. Always follow the leading of the Holy Spirit. When a believer prays he is not talking with his best buddy he is addressing The LORD God Almighty! Be respectful! Be VERY RESPECTFUL!

# CHAPTER 19

# PRAYER LIST

A PRAYER LIST CAN BE BOTH good and bad at the same time. Come again. By using a prayer list as a reminder, you can make sure you pray for everything and everybody that you think needs prayer. No one and no need should be carelessly overlooked. You told people that you would pray for them and you did. A careless omission can leave you with a serious unmet need. If you think that you have prayed for everything and everyone, then it is easy for you to skip over one of the main functions of prayer, fellowship with the Father. You also need to be sensitive the prodding's of the Holy Spirit who may want you to pray about other needs and concerns.

Another problem with a prayer list is that it is very easy to let your well-meaning list become a chant with very little spiritual value. It's easy to say the same things over and over and loose awareness that you are in the throne room of Almighty God. This is dangerous in that the quality of your prayers can easily backslide into statements of a lower quality and from there down into an even less effective area. NOTE 1: An excellent prayer is not rated so by its eloquence or correct grammar. Quality here is a purely a spiritual attribute.

Prayer lists are one of the most common formats that people use when praying. As of yet, I haven't found a Biblical statement advocating their use. At the same time, I also haven't found a Scripture condemning their use. Does that mean that it is up to the person who is praying to choose his prayer practice? Maybe yes, maybe no. I would suggest that if a believer is aware of the possible problems that can be associated with a written list and is able to avoid them without being distracted, then it is not only okay but desirable to use them.

At this point the millions of believers who use a prayer list may be starting to become unglued. Let us consider the negatives before we reject them.

When a person uses a prayer list consistently by reading off the same request one by one each day the list eventually becomes memorized. From this point praying can easily seep into a habit where a person repeats the same words quickly without thinking about what he is praying for and whom he is praying to. As time progresses their prayer can become like a chant, a chant can easily become a meaningless group of sounds. Hence, prayer can become a staged task. Another chore that one can mark off of his "things to do" list. In this case the person praying could just as well point to the list and ask the good LORD to do or bless whoever or whatever is on the list. This is not praying!

On the positive side the sincere believer who uses his list as a reminder to pray for someone and follows the leading of God's Holy Spirit is using his list correctly. For example, if you have promised a lot of people that you would pray for them each day, then this is a positive way that you can keep that promise. If you choose to use a prayer list, be on guard that you don't let it slip into a non-spiritual routine. It is very easy to slip; especially when you have a very long list, you get in a hurry or you are tired. Prayer is not a timed task. Prayer time should be as free from outward events and pressures as possible. Feel free to depart from the list as the Holy Spirit moves you. You will likely end up praying for many things and people that are not on your list. In the same spirit, when you are led to drop or add a name to your list or to modify a request, do so. Always follow the Holy Spirit's leadings.

All believers who pray have this obligation in common. They need to be praying in harmony with God's Holy Spirit. Scriptures clearly indicate that the Holy Spirit helps the believer pray. Always rely on God's Spirit. He will let you know when to pray, what to pray, and how to pray. He will help you align your requests so that they are in agreement with God's will. Trust Him!

"Likewise the Spirit helps us in our weakness. For we do not know what to pray for as we ought, but the Spirit himself intercedes for us with groanings too deep for words. And he who searches hearts knows what is the mind of the Spirit, because the Spirit intercedes for the saints according to the will of God."

Romans 8:26-27

When a person is not praying "in the Spirit", are they praying?

# CHAPTER 20

# ASKING OTHERS TO PRAY FOR YOUR NEEDS

CERTAIN PRAYERS SHOULD BE PRIVATE. Other prayer needs are appropriate to share with special believing friends. Some prayer requests are appropriate for larger groups of believers. Which is which and how should they be handled? NOTE 1: There are some appropriate prayers for unbelievers to request.

> **"Again I say to you, if two of you agree on earth about anything they ask, it will be done for them by my Father in heaven."**
>
> Matthew 18:19

The only important guideline is to follow the leading of the Holy Spirit. The problem is that in intense situations we are often overwhelmed and are not fully acting under the leadership of God's Spirit as we know we should. Many times, in dire emergencies we revert back to our old nature. Even then, we often know enough to make imperative prayer requests. NOTE 2: In the times when we may not be fully acting under the control of the Holy Spirit, God still loves us. He is constantly taking actions that are for our betterment. Many times, we are not aware of all the wonderful things that He is doing unless He chooses to show His hand to us. The believer who is under the control of the Holy Spirit will be more aware of God's activities much quicker than those who are less concerned about His will.

The ability to quickly ask more believers to pray for you is one of the benefits of belonging to a local church. There you will have more believing friends and more ways of contacting them. In emergency situations you can easily and quickly contact several Christians so that they can pray for your urgent pressing request. Churches also give you the privilege of knowing about and praying for the needs of others who need your prayers.

> NOTE 3: Some people have to travel in their job. They should, as best as they can, associate with a believing Church at whatever location they find themselves in. Rely on the Holy Spirit for guidance. They might not be your flavor of Christianity but do the best you can. There are believers in almost every Church that proclaims to be Christian. Should you end up visiting in a church with zero or very few believers then you might have a special assignment there.

Normally, there are standard ways for church members to request prayers. In some churches it is the practice for people who pray or want someone to pray for them to attend prayer meetings and as part of the program there is usually a time for prayer requests. If you are unable to be present you could contact your pastor and ask for his prayers and you can ask him to make the request for you at a prayer meeting. NOTE 4: Sometimes a pastor may believe that your request should be private. If you want him to share it with others, you should clearly express that to him. In many churches there are group meetings at one time they were called Sunday school classes. Here you will get to know more believers on a closer and more personal level. Even in choir practice sessions there will normally be times for prayer and an opportunity to request prayer.

Many churches have a formal program for listing prayer request. They often make efforts to conform to the HIPAA laws (HIPAA: An Acronym that stands for the Health Insurance Portability and Accountability Act, a US law designed to provide privacy standards to protect patients' medical records.) Normally, you need to contact your church and specifically ask that your request is added to the church's prayer list for those members who choose to pray for the prayer needs of others. Follow your church's procedures.

The internet also provides various means of making prayer requests. Be careful. Some users of the internet may be acting as direct agents of Satan. If they hear that you are going to the hospital, they may try to break into your home. Some people might even use your request as a seed for gossip. Be prudent.

The method I choose is to write a series of email letters and send copies (BCC) only to the ones that I want to be praying for me. When I do this, I print out an extra copy for a prayer warrior that I know does not use the internet. After mentioning your concerns be sure to make it clear that you want God's will to be done above everything else. There is nothing better! The following is a series of these emails. Some parts were deleted for HIPAA and other necessary reasons: This series of prayers began shortly after a surgery.

*I think I have recovered to most of my normal level of sanity, if I haven't, I probably wouldn't know it. Please excuse **any dumb** statements, typos, misspellings, etc.*

*The hospital was slow in contacting my cousin. He finally was able to get up with me. I needed to exercise a small part of one of my gifts. A gift that I don't like to use: **expediting**. Ask me later and I will tell you about how I discovered that I had this gift. Anyway, Dr. xxxx will be calling my cousin, xxx, in the morning, Dr. xxxx is probably waiting for test results to come back.*

*It is my present understanding that he removed several adhesions, he believes that this will allow me to eat more foods (A big improvement over my liquid diet). My pain level is good. If I am still, I can barely detect it, if I move, it discourages movement. They are using a nerve bock instead of Opioids. It works much better. But they will be doing this for only the first 72 hours. Then the other pain relievers will be used if needed. Consequently, some of them will discourage the small intestine from functioning at its normal speed.*

*Backspacing, I arrived at the hospital ahead of schedule at 5:50 AM this morning. I was feeling fine. From the front door to the elevator that led to the operating area was about a 300-yard walk. This place is huge. It is about xx blocks long by x blocks wide and growing. I heard the shuttle driver say that it was rated as the number x hospital in the US. They have xxxxx employees. It is also rated number x in several areas.*

*Some of my problems are: My mouth is very dry and so are my lips. Doctors here and everywhere else that I have been have seemed to resist hydrating me to the amount that I want. There is probably a good reason for this. The other concern is more problematic. When I was at XXX my small intestine stopped working after surgery, the doctor said my small intestine was shy. It acted like it wanted to just crawl into a hole and rest. This lasted for several days. They started off with the same feeding schedule here, liquids, Jell-O, broth etc. This progresses to soft foods etc. Today, I ate the Jell-O, and drank a small amount of tea. I noticed what I think, are some early symptoms of "shyness". I am now trying to avoid this. These are things you can pray about!*

*The thing that surprised me was that as I went from place to place I noticed that all of the patients that I saw were normal working people. I was expecting to see limo's all over the place. The walls here, as large as it is, have a lot of good quality art. This place is very special.*

*Another prayer request: After 72 hours they may need to put me on Opioids. They will slow down the intestine awakening process. Pray as you feel led.*

*I will write more as things change and as I am able too. I presently feel good and I am being treated well. All of my physical needs are being taken care of. All I need is prayer.*

### *May God's will be done!*

*Today, I have lots of good things to write about. In my late night e-mail I listed my requests. Three people responded by very early this morning. There is a verse that says that before you ask that the good LORD will answer, it has been demonstrated to me that this is very true. Another* verse goes along with this one it states that the prayers of the righteous availed much.

Last night I asked for prayers about several concerns.

This morning I started seeing some of the results.

I was very concerned with my small intestine going shy. At 11:07 PM on Aug. 14 I noticed some movements. Around 1:30 this morning the bag needed to be emptied. This morning around 6:00 AM when Dr. xxxx came be to see me He looked at the bag and it needed emptying again. Twenty minutes later his fellow (a fellow is a fully trained doctor who is similar to an apprentice under the guidance of a very accomplished and skilled doctor) came by and he wanted to see the bag. It had more in it. The small intestine is coming out of hiding. I don't know how much. When I have eaten some more, I will probably find out. This is still a concern but there is reason to believe that it is improving.

Generally speaking, I am feeling better.

Dr. xxxx was able to safely remove a few of the adhesions, some are still there. He said it would have been too risky to deal with all of them. However, enough have been removed that Dr. xxxx thinks that I will be able to eat more different foods. His fellow told me that I will probably have some plug ups. But I have had some experience dealing with and avoiding them. Please pray for wisdom, good counseling, and for fewer problems.

My pain level which was not very high, is nearly zero, when I am still. When I move a little it is a little less painful than it was yesterday. Things are improving. Thank you Jesus! My mouth is not as dry as it was and my lips are getting better. Another praise.

I have already talked with some very smart specialists. Already they have told me things that will be helpful. These specialists have mentioned others in their field that are even more specially trained. I still have other problems that I would like for them to address. Please pray for the counseling and treatment that I need but I didn't come here primarily to see them.

I sense that this cycle of improvements started several months ago when at the end of the church service I went down to the front and someone prayed with me generally for improvements in my condition. I believe the blockages that I had that sent me to the ER were part of His plan. The tests that they did, that I didn't think were necessary. The lady hospitalists' whom I had never seen before, who had me admitted were also part of His plan too. The surgeon that she referred me to, who backed out of doing the surgery, motivated me to seek Dr. xxxx's advice on who should do the surgery and then he offered to do it. All of this, I believe was part of Gods leading that got me here. God is GOOD!

Please continue to pray that I will not need the opioids. And pray as you are led. God's will is much better than any of us can imagine.

Thank you for your prayers.


Not very much is happening today. On the other hand, I sense that I am making good improvements. One of the activities is getting out of bed and walking. This afternoon I made three rounds in the hall ways between the nursing stations and the patients' rooms. (The nurse only expected one round.) In order to do this, I have to get out of bed first. This normally involves a twisting stress on the torso. This produces pain. (NOTE: Pain can be your friend, it helps one to know when to stop or modify an activity so that he doesn't hurt himself.) I can now with very minimal help get out of bed. I still need a little more help to get back in bed. Another activity is eating. They still have me on a liquid diet. This is an area of concern.

If I eat solid food too soon or too much or something with too much consistency, there can be problems. They have solutions to these problems. I had these problems at XXX and don't want to repeat them. Complicating things, the nerve block will be wearing off soon. It is rated at 72 hours beginning around 8:30 AM on the 14th. After this, if there is pain, the solution is Opioids. They take care of the pain but they slow down the small intestine. This can lead to digestion problems. Please pray about this.

On the better side: I am part of a study on the two different ways of doing nerve blocks. They want to know which one is best and *which one should be best used on which patient. Today, a lady in the research group came by and ask me some questions for statically purposes, like pain levels etc. I tried to give her answers that could be used statically. Anyway, at the end of the discussion I told her that statically speaking she might want to throw my answers out because I am part of a different universe (a statistical term, it doesn't imply that I could be from Mars).*

*Getting to the point, I told her that a large number of people were praying for me, (verses the other people who may have had just the normal amount of lukewarm prayers), When she left, she said God bless you. She may be a believer or at a minimum, at least somewhat familiar with Christianity. Please pray for their team when they discuss this that she will be able to give some level of testimony. And that it is received in a good manner.*

*Another upcoming event will relate to going home. I will need to be able to pass through the TSA inspection. I will likely have a chest full of stainless-steel medical staples. Please pray about this. I probably will not be writing a note every day, just when there are changes or prayer concerns.*

*PS*

*Yesterday, I told Mrs. xxxxx one of my favorite verses, "And it came to pass". Last night when her family was getting ready to leave she quoted it to them.*

*Breakfast was an upgrade from liquids to grits and bacon. Lunch was Salmon. The first Salmon I have had in a long time. Thou this is very desirable. It is also a test. Prior to the surgery food would accumulate before it plugged me up. Tonight, I have selected Cod. Now the unknown is if food will slightly fill the intestines and start coming out the other end. If it doesn't then the surgery did not accomplish as much as we thought it would do. If it does come out OK, the next test will be more foods. If I push solid foods too far, I will be plugged up. If this happens, hopefully I will be able to wait it out like I have been doing. I should know in a few days how successful the surgery was.*

*At noon today the nurse came by and removed the hydration needle. I am no longer on a tether. This is a big step toward flying home to Charlotte.*

*I have prepared a list of functions that I need to be able to do before I get discharged. From discharge I will go to a hotel, for two days; then, if I am OK I will catch the next flight to Charlotte. Once here I will have the guidelines that I will need to follow for about six weeks. Around this time, I should be as close to my new normal as I can be.*

*Things needing prayer: Being able to eat without plugging up, wound healing, pain treatment without Opioids, traveling mercies, and doctor's good judgments regarding lessor matters. Above all else: Please pray the God's will is done!*

*Last night, while flossing a crown on a tooth popped off. Life happens.*

*Rarely does something complex go forth without a snag. Recovery is one of these. Yesterday was my snag number one. I was upgraded to solid food. I purposefully tried to not eat everything on my plate, because of past problems. Well, the past problems happened anyway. Last night I had some digestive problems. I called the nurse and she checked things over. Because I had similar problems before, we decided that I should try to walk it out. I walked for about and fifty minutes. This helped and later on the blockage was relieved.*

*Today, the stoma nurse visited me and she taught me about the new bag, its use and components. She was one of the people I wanted to talk to. She went over the new bag and showed me what I needed to know. I was also able to discuss my invention with her without telling her how it worked. (She understood the patent process and some of the relevant laws and she referred me to the company that makes the new bag. Since I am looking for a company to partner with me in turning this prototype into a desirable and patented product.) NOTE: This invention will make it possible for many people with bags to be able to sleep all night without having to check their bag to see if it needed to be emptied. (If you don't understand the reason for this you can ask me after I get back to Charlotte.) Being able to sleep is a very good activity.*

*This afternoon I saw the physical therapist. We went over the things that I would need to be able to do before they let me go to the hotel. I can do some of them now. The hardest one is to be able to get into and out of a flatbed without help. The next visit from her will probably be on Wednesday. If I go to the hotel Wednesday and spent Wednesday and Thursday nights there; then, Friday would be the earliest time I could be back. It is possible that I will be back at church on Sunday. At this time, I don't know for sure. I hope to see you soon.*

*Mr. xxxx is getting extra care and seems to be getting better. Please continue to pray for both of us.* ***There is nothing better than God's will being done!***

*I just got off the phone with Ms. xxxxx, the Concierge at the xxxx hospital. I now have a good rate and a room reservation at the hotel near the hospital for Wed. and Thursday nights. Friday morning sometime, I will need to go by Dr. xxxx's office and get the staples removed; then off to the airport. She has also booked my flight back to Charlotte, I am scheduled to be back there around 6:51 PM. These are prayer items!!! Any little change can throw everything out of kilter. A lot can happen between now and then.*

*I should arrive in Charlotte physically better than I was when I left. I am eating better already. From past experience I know that some problems may take days to develop. Please pray about these too. I am looking forward to being in Church Sunday. God is good!*


*I am out. I have been physically improved in several ways. I stayed later than I had planned. After I finished going over some details of my future self-care with 3 different nurses I had supper, packed, and I rode the shuttle over to the Holiday Inn. (about a half mile away from my room). When I got to the room I looked out the window and no more* than 10 feet away there was the Stares and Strips waving in the breeze. Tomorrow I have nothing scheduled. Friday morning, I will get up and pack most of my stuff. I will contact the desk and they will call the shuttle to Dr. xxxx's office. My appointment is for 8:30 AM. I will see Dr. xxxx and someone will remove the staples and we will go over my next appointments, Etc. When we finish I will see the ostomy nurse. When that's finished I will eat breakfast in the same building as Dr. xxxx's office. Then it is back to the hotel. I will get ready and pack. And call transportation. I will check out around 2:00 PM. I will be eating light so that I want have to empty the bag on the plane. Needless to say. This can be very difficult in a small compartment. I will check my luggage and go through TSA screening. Ms. xxxxx, the Concierge at the xxxxxx hospital did a wonderful job setting up everything.

Don will be picking me up at the airport in Charlotte around sundown. Being here has been a great adventure. Everyone has treated me with respect and kindness in addition to the very best of medical care. It's not over yet. With this schedule there are lots of possibilities for problems. While I want a smooth trip my prayer request is constant. Please pray for God's will to be done. NOTHING IS BETTER!

Around 11:00 PM I noticed a little plug up in my left ear. I took some Afrin.


Nothing is as simple and as easy as it should be, especially when there is a Spiritual aspect to it. I went by to see Dr. xxxx. He had someone remove the staples, ouch, it wasn't too bad but the feeling was not desirable. Anyway, we discussed the next steps. He wants me to keep him informed and I will be seeing several of my NC doctors for their yearly check-ups. The nurse had told me not to drive for 2 weeks. (**ALLWAYS APPEAL A DECISION YOU DON'T LIKE!!!**) I asked Dr. xxxx about this. He was concerned with me feeling pain and being distracted by it when I applied the brakes. He suggested that I start with a short trip around the neighborhood or a local store for a start. Then increasing it gradually. I will try it this afternoon. If I have problems, I will contact one of you *for a ride. While on the plane I simulated this by pushing against the seat support on the seat in front of me on the plane. NO pain.*

*Next, I visited the cafeteria in the same building as Dr. xxxx's office. I looked at all of the many choices and decided to take a chance on a strange object. I asked what it was. It was called a pizza roll. It looked more like a Danish. It was very tasty! Then, I got on the shuttle and went to the one drug store on their route. I got some Flonase and some Poly-grip. (A retired nurse friend wrote me and said that it works well as a temporary replacement glue for a crown. It does.) I went back to my room and finished packing and waited for the Limo. Ms. xxxxx had asked the owner of the limo service to take care of me. He did a good job and got the "helpers" at the airport to finish the job. Finally, they rolled me on the plane. The journey was almost over, or so I thought. (A Spiritual battle never ends!!) Up, up and away. I was on my way home. I had an aisle seat and a 40-ish gentleman sat by me. The plane pushed off 6 minutes early. We taxied out to the active runway. I noticed that we were taxing very slowly. Soon the plane stopped and the pilot announced that the FAA had put a temporary hold on us due to weather in Charlotte. After about 30 minutes we started moving.*

*As we flew, the other guy was occupied with his computer game but we chatted a little bit. As he talked he casually mentioned that he lived in xxxxxx and **xxxx** was expecting him. Gulp. It didn't take much discernment to identify a problem. I prayed silently, I wanted to help him spiritually. All I received was that he had already crossed the line and that I couldn't help him. Nevertheless, I prayed that the Good LORD would give him at least one more chance.*

*I noticed that the pilot was doing slow figure eights, we were in a holding pattern. He finally announced that we were delayed for landing due to the local weather. He said that when it cleared we would be first since we were at the lowest altitude. After a considerable time, the pilot announced that due to low fuel we would be landing in Asheville. Everyone seemed to be discussing the possibilities. We landed. The fuel*

*truck was prompt and the fueling was over shortly. We waited. I*
*we took off and flew 19 minutes and landed in Charlotte. We u*
*the far west runway. Our pilot taxied very slowly. We ended u*
*gate 25 of the commuter airlines. Because they used a wheel chair*
*me on and I had some carry –on luggage. Walking the distance w.*
*a good idea. I waited. Finally, a person who pushed wheel chairs a*
*and she hurried me on my way. Finally, we got to Don. He ha*
*luggage and we went to his SUV. The ride home was good. We ar*
*about midnight. It was a long day.*

*This morning I unpacked and started the clean-up process. I*
*out and got the paper and was able to do my Tai Chi, Simplified*
*Style. I did it twice. NO pain! I did it slower than my normal, but*
*is the way it is supposed to be done. I hope to see many of you at Chu*
*tomorrow!*


*I am doing fine for this step in my healing. My next thing to overco*
*relates to one of the drugs that I have been taking for the last 5 yea*
*Its purpose was to slow down the small intestines so that it could abso*
*water for hydration. The xxxx xxxx has developed another way*
*optimizing hydration. I have started it and have reduce the meds l*
*25%, so far. If I can eliminate all of this drug. I should have othe*
*benefits that are well worth the effort.*

*I am gradually increasing my low-level aerobics at the gym.*
*have been at the gym 10 times since my release date. No pain and n*
*problems. After the end of the month, I will be cleared for some of my*
*weight bearing exercises. Then in another 6 weeks I will have no more*
*restrictions.*

*In October I will be seeing three of my regular doctors for follow*
*up exams.*

*Please continue to remember me in your prayers. There is always the*
*possibility of the unexpected.*
*Thank you*

*On Tuesday I had a MRI and an ARI the results came back very good! Today Bob and I drove to XXX for my yearly check-up. There I had a different MRI and in order to do it they did a Creatine test first. The Creatine test was the best one I have had in a long time. The MRI showed no problems and within their measuring error the dimensions were 1mm smaller than last year. These tests were done for another purpose. Dr. xxxx told me that they could be done in place of a follow up visit for my surgery. He said I did not need to come back unless I have problems. I am almost wordless. All I can say is* **THANK YOU JESUS!**
**Thank you for your many prayers!**

By using this means of making prayer request you have reasonable control over your information. It is also relatively easy to write different messages for different people. For example, you may choose to go into more detailed descriptions concerning your prayer request for your family. For believers you may know at work you might choose to give them some of the content or an abbreviated request. It is your option. Request prayers wisely. You may even choose to send copies to weak believers or to persons that are just friends. This way when the Good LORD answers the request, a seed of faith may be planted where it can do some good. How else are they going to be made aware of your Heavenly Father's work in your life? Without your email they could just assume that you somehow got lucky.

Instead of writing just one email that covers everything, I prefer to do it in sequential stages as things develop. As each of the smaller needs are handled, I send out updates with the next concerns? With each update it is important to express thanks for the prayers and for God's interventions. It is important and an act of faith building to learn that the concerns that you have been praying for have been blessed by the Good LORD.

The obvious question arises. Why should I send some copies to friends who are not believers? Am I counting on their "prayers" to help me? The answer is simple. Answered prayer tends to increase

the faith in the one who prays. Some people need to see multiple demonstrations of faith (in others) in order for them to understand that there is a God and that He does answer prayers.

> **"But without faith it is impossible to please him: for he that cometh to God must believe that he is, and that he is a rewarder of them that diligently seek him."**
>
> Hebrews 11:6KJV

Unbelieving friends are still friends. They want to know what is going on. They will be concerned. Some may think, "What if this were to happen to me?" They will see you and how you reacted. Some may even visit you. Do they see a frantic person at their wits end or do they see a believer peacefully waiting on the GOOD LORD?

Well written prayer requests are clear and provide good benefits for you and numerous opportunities for leading others closer to the Master.

# CHAPTER 21

# HOW SHOULD A BELIEVER
# RESPOND TO A PRAYER REQUEST

You are discussing something with a friend, co-worker or a total stranger and they either ask if you will pray for them or somehow indicate that they need pray. How do you react? Well-uh, you promise to pray for them. Sometimes this is all that you think that you need to do. But is it? When there are dire compelling needs, many times the best thing you can do is to instantly start praying, out loud, for the person and the need that is so troubling them.

One time when I was visiting in a distant city the Moslem cab driver mentioned that he was having a hard time finding a suitable place for his family to live. I ask him if I could pray for his need. He consented. I prayed for him out loud and in Jesus's name. He was so stunned that he couldn't open his mouth. Perhaps that was the first time he had an encounter with a Christian where he was introduced to a believing prayer. I will probably never know the result of this prayer. I suspect that he will not forget it either. I am trusting the Holy Spirit to remind him of this prayer when he secures a good home for his family.

NOTE 1: This kind of prayer can be a most memorable prayer, both for you and for them. For many people this could be the first time someone has prayed for them out loud and in person.

Pray in the Spirit when you venture forth into this area. Oftentimes this is the front line in spiritual warfare. This will most likely be an intense prayer. Later, when you are alone pray again, ask God's Spirit to guide both you and the other person.

After praying for him there is often something tangible that you can do and many times should do. Trust the leading of God's Spirit. He may lead you to give him some money, He may lead you to do some good work. He may also lead you to offer physical help with a problem. Many times there is some advice that you can give that will be beneficial. When you pray for someone, be alert to the messages that the Holy Spirit may be sending you. In some cases, you may hold the answer to their heart felt needs. …. In all cases Jesus does!

Take prayer request seriously, when you are watching the news on TV and they show a distressing scene and someone asks for the viewers to pray for them. PRAY! If you don't pray, it could count against you. Sometimes the Father doesn't act until someone prays. When you delay praying for someone in need, you may be delaying a Devine action that they desperately need. Remember, you can always pray for God's will to be done. There is no better prayer.

Another time you may be driving on a routine trip to the grocery store and someone cuts in front of you almost causing an accident. The temptation to say harsh words will be pressing upon you. Instead of making profane statements, why not pray for them and thank the good LORD for keeping them and you safe. Just because their way of making a prayer request is a bit different, it doesn't reduce your praying obligations. Make it a practice to always pray for the other driver.

When a believer gets his spiritual mind in tune with the Holy Spirit he will become aware of many more needs and opportunities for prayer. While some might say that praying is the least you can do. It is, in fact, the most that you can do.

How do the unsaved express their need for prayer? Don't worry. They will make it obvious. If they don't specifically request that you pray for their need, pray a quick silent prayer for God's Spirit to guide you. Sometimes He will guide you to pray out loud, sometimes He will guide you in how to best pray for them, and many times He may lead you to do something. Wherever The Spirit leads, you should go. Whatever He says to do, you should do. When He says don't do something, **<u>OBEY HIM</u>**!

## CHAPTER 22

# IMPERATIVE PRAYER OBLIGATIONS

BELIEVERS HAVE CLEAR-CUT PRAYER OBLIGATIONS. When we fail to pray for these, we are out of God's will. The Father expects believers to do many things. He created each of us for a distinct purpose. He has reasons for each of our assignments. The believer's only important earthly activity is to do His will!

One of the most overlooked prayer responsibilities is for each of us is to have fellowship time with the Father. Part of this fellowship is that we spend time doing things together with Him. Anything that He wants us to do is something that needs to be done. He also wants us to help and work with other believers in order accomplish His will. In many cases it is difficult to do His will without involving others.

When we are truly doing His will, the Holy Spirit is guiding, directing, and empowering us so that the LORD's work will be done in the manner that He wants it done. The most imperative prayer obligation for any believer is to give his full attention and obedience to the Holy Spirit.

Any time we think that we are doing the LORD's will all by ourselves we are on an ego trip! When we choose freely to do God's will by following the leading of the Holy Spirit we are recognizing our place in the Father's overall plans. That is why we were created. NOTE 1: Prayer is communication with the Father. Communication is a two-way event.

> NOTE 2: It is possible for two people to be physically doing acts that appear to be identical. No one can't see, hear, or in any non-spiritual way detect any difference in what they are doing. One could be doing it under the leadership of the Holy

Spirit and the other could only be exercising his free will. The long-term results will be different. One will have accomplished God's will, while the other person may have just thought that he was doing something that God expected him to do. At the best he performed a good deed.

NOTE 3: The word "act" has at least two meanings. In this case both meanings apply. 1. Act can mean that a person did something. 2. In this case the second meaning is more accurate. He did something like an actor in a play. In this mode the person pretended to do something without the leading and underlying support of the Holy Spirit. The result is that he expended energy and accomplished nothing of lasting spiritual value. The other person prayed and followed the leading of God's Holy Spirit. He followed the leading of the LORD. He not only accomplished God's will but he laid up for himself heavenly rewards. He did God's will. The options are prayerfully submitting to God's Spirit or alternatively doing a "good deed" and hoping to impress other earthlings. The latter choice leaves God out and places the entire burden on the actor's shoulders.

Another prayer obligation is to pray for everyone who ask us to pray for them. Every time someone ask for prayer believers should pray for them. This includes people on the news broadcast who are being interviewed and ask for prayer. For believers this is a serious obligation.

Our prayer may not be the one they wanted. A believer's prayer should always include specifically asking for God's will to be done. There is nothing better.

Another major obligation is to pray for the salvation of the lost. Any time our spirit is moved by the Holy Spirit to believe that someone may be lost we should pray for their salvation.

Anytime we see a prayer answered or sense the help of the Holy Spirit we should offer a prayer of thanksgiving. NOTE 4: When a person is not thankful he is taking the first step toward backsliding!

One of the most overlooked prayers is to pray for those in authority. This includes the boss that we don't like, even if we have a good reason, for political leaders, even when we strongly disagree with them. We are subject to lots of people: police, mayors, senators, other representatives' various bureaucrats, the flight crew on a plane that we are traveling on. The list is very long.

> **"First of all, then, I urge that supplications, prayers, intercessions, and thanksgivings be made for all people, for kings and all who are in high positions, that we may lead a peaceful and quite life, godly and dignified in every way. This is good, and it is pleasing in the sight of God our Savior, who desires all people to be saved and to come to the knowledge of the truth."**

> I Timothy 2:1-4

Finally, anytime we are personally faced with a challenge or need to choose between alternatives no matter how easy or how difficult it might be, we should pray. We should specifically ask the Father to lead and empower us to do His will His way, in His perfect time, with His strength and with the attitude that represents His leading. Someone is always watching us. Always be a good example of a believer who is choosing to be under the Lordship of the Master! Attitudes are important!

One could very well ask," Why are these imperative obligations for believers?" This question can be answered with a few other questions: How else can I express my thanks to the Almighty for the many things that He has done for me? How else can I know what He wants me to do? After He saves individuals why doesn't He instantly carry them to heaven to be with Him? The answer is simple. He has things that He wants each of us to do on earth. He chooses to use prayer, Bible study, and the Holy Spirit as the normal means of communicating our assignments to us.

When we fail in our prayer obligations, we are not only hurting ourselves. We are setting ourselves up for a correction. The Good LORD is not slack. He loves us so much that He is willing for us to undergo hardship when the result of this can lead us into a closer fellowship with Him. Difficulties can also put us into a position where He can bless us and use us as a witness to others.

# CHAPTER 23

# BECOMING EQUIPPED TO BE HOLY

The Good LORD didn't just give us an encyclopedia of rules and obligations and tell us to keep them. He has offered us a considerable supply of Spiritual tools and He gave us instructions on how to get and apply them through prayer and Bible study. The good LORD has instructed us in His Word about the kind and nature of the spiritual tools. Utilizing them is necessary in order to determine and do His will. His spiritual tools and the help of the Holy Spirit multiply our spiritual abilities exponentially. All spiritual resources can be traced back to The Holy Bible. They are put to use through heart felt prayers that are guided by the Holy Spirit.

**"Put on the whole armor of God, that you may be able to stand against the schemes of the devil. For we do not wrestle against flesh and blood, but against the rulers, against the authorities, against the cosmic powers over this present darkness, against the spiritual forces of evil in the heavenly places. Therefore, take up the whole armor of God, that you may be able to withstand in the evil day, and having done all, to stand firm. Stand therefore, having fastened on the belt of truth, and having put on the breastplate of righteousness, and as shoes for your feet, having put on the readiness given by the gospel of peace. In all circumstances take up the shield of faith, with which you can extinguish all the flaming darts of the evil one; and take the helmet of salvation,**

**and the sword of the Spirit, which is the
word of God, praying at all times in the
Spirit, with all prayer and supplications. To
that end keep alert with all perseverance,
making supplications for all the saints,
and also for me, that words may be given
to me in opening my mouth boldly to
proclaim the mystery of the gospel,"**

Ephesians 6:11-19

Satan is the believer's adversary. He is constantly scheming and using his resources to disrupt believers. Apparently he has two main objectives: 1. Keeping the lost, lost. And 2. Keeping believers from doing God's will. In our own human strength, no one is able by himself to successfully resist his attacks. NB: One of his favorite schemes is to cause someone to think that he has personally, all by himself, conquered a particular sin. When this happens, he is just setting him up for a much deeper life of sin.

On the other hand, there is consistent victory available for the believer who is in God's will. Regrettably, many believers aren't familiar with the battle plan nor do they appropriate the spiritual resources that can make victory doable. Many believers accept spiritual defeats as normal! Ignorance of the Word is expensive.

Whatever Satan's schemes are, the Good LORD has provided the appropriate weapons to defeat them. The LORD's well equipped armory is available to all believers. The armory is described in His Word. Victory is simple and always possible but it is not always easy. Victory requires spiritual strength and energy that are gained only through Bible study, prayer, fellowship with the Father and Spirit enabled obedience.

The first armament that is mentioned in Ephesians 6:14 is **the belt of truth.** This truth is the wisdom that is contained in the Holy Bible. Read it. Study it. And apply it. The belt holds everything together. It keeps your sword handy and provides basic body support. Truth also serves similar spiritual purposes. Without the truth of God's Word, in the believer's heart, the string of thoughts that lead to spiritual victories is broken. When a believer doesn't use these tools Satan often leads him toward defective beliefs, wrong assumptions and spiritual weakness. Flawed conclusions produce defective actions. Wrong actions result in defeat. Defeat draws one closer to death! God's truth is vital for every believer.

The next protection is the **breastplate of righteousness,** Ephesians 6:14. In warfare the driving force is to kill the enemy before he can kill you. When a person's heart is vulnerable their life is in danger. This is especially true in the spiritual world. When your heart is not protected by the righteousness described in God's Word, you are on the road to spiritual defeat. Protect your heart by acquiring and maintaining the righteousness that can only be found in the Holy Bible.

These Scriptures use the symbolism of the military equipment of a Roman solder to illustrate some basic spiritual truths. Someone might ask, why do they include **shoes for your feet,** Ephesians 6:15? In any physical struggle the feet are very important. When a person loses their footing they fall and become very vulnerable. It is very difficult to fight while lying down. The feet also serve other purposes. They can remove us from danger and when we are led by the Holy Spirit and they can move a person through perilous places where the Gospel needs to be proclaimed.

The next tool of spiritual warfare is **the readiness given by the gospel of peace,** Ephesians 6:15. This is the confidence that a believer has when his life is saturated with the Holy Scriptures. When a person has God's Word in his heart and in his thoughts he is in an optimum position to hear and follow God's instructions. For the Believer his level of closeness to the Father is proportional to the quality of his prayer life. When we follow Jesus it is a Spiritual victory.

In any spiritual struggle we can expect the enemy to fight with every means that he can muster. The **shield of faith,** Ephesians 6:16. is our defense against everything that the enemy can throw at us. NOTE: Even in physical conflicts there is always an underlying spiritual battle.

The last piece of defensive armor mentioned is **the helmet of salvation,** Ephesians 6:17. When the head is damaged there is no more battle. For the believer the ultimate victory is already won. Everything else is related to how we demonstrate to others the difference that Jesus has made in our lives.

The only offensive weapon that a believer has is **sword of the Spirit, which is the Word of God,** Ephesians 6:17. This weapon is most effective when it is embedded in our heart and projected through our lives and our mouths. The disgrace of our age is that so many of us go through the battles of life too ill equipped to win even a minor skirmish.

Some may wonder, if I am chasing rabbits down a cold trail, when I refer to the Full armor of God in a book on prayer. On the contrary, the various armors of God are all critical and all of them depend on Spirit led prayers. How else can you put on spiritual armor?

1. Through prayer the Holy Spirit confirms and teaches The Word to the believer. A non-believer could read the Bible all day long and never get the high level of **truth** from it that a believer could receive in a short time.
2. No one can ever hope to become **righteous** unless he first prays sincere forgiveness prayers.
3. A person's **shoes** are his prime method of transportation. Without prayer it would be very difficult for a believer to be where the Father wants him to be. Sometimes the road is very rough and potentially dangerous. Shoes are also helpful when someone steps on our spiritual toes. Through prayer we are directed where the LORD wants us to go.
4. **The gospel of peace**, is what the believer brings to the world. In frightful times and perilous journeys, the believer

only needs to pray and receive the spiritual comfort that only the Good LORD can provide. This comfort is for both himself and the people that he influences. A believer can through prayer ask the Holy Spirit to protect and to bring peace into his heart.

5. **The shield of faith** is the result of the believer experiencing answers to prayer. Every time a believer prays and experiences answered prayer his faith is strengthened. When was the last time you trusted God for something that He delivered?

6. **The helmet of salvation** can only be secured by prayer. Re. "Dear LORD please forgive me of my sins and let me live with you forever in heaven. AMEN"

7. **The sword of the Spirit, which is the word of God** can only be effectively used by a believer who is communicating with the Holy Spirit. Communicating with the Holy Spirit is always a prayer function.

Every facet of a victorious Christian life depends on prayer! ....

# HOW DO YOU THANK THE ALMIGHTY? - PART 1

You sense that the good LORD has done something that is beneficial for you. How do you express appreciation to the Almighty? Can you just bow your head and say, "Thank you for everything that you have done for me, everything that you are currently doing for me, and everything you will be doing for me. AMEN!" And let that be it. Does that really satisfy your need to demonstrate gratitude to the GOOD LORD? I sincerely hope that no one reading this would think that voicing such empty words would be a valid way of thanking the good LORD.

Most of us probably came to the same conclusion very quickly. Just pronouncing the words "Thank You" is not sufficient. Not even when you are thanking another human being, much less the Creator of the Universe, but I would suggest that every one of us at one time or another has done the very same thing, or unfortunately much less. We only spoke the words, "thank you" to the one who died a miserable death so that we could have a victorious life and that we wouldn't have to spend eternity in never ending punishment!

This brings up an obvious question. Is prayer more than saying some meaningful words? Let us explore the possibilities. Let's say that with all of the things that the good LORD is doing for us that we are able to recognize that one of them is special and we pray a sincere prayer of thanksgiving, as best we can. Well, that is certainly better, but what about the many other good things that He is doing for us other than the one thing that we thanked Him for.

Going a little further, is it humanly possible for a believer to properly and completely thank his heavenly Father for everything that He has so generously done for him? One thing that we should add to the thank you prayer is a thankful attitude. Through His divine nature he continues to give us the things that He wants us to have. These are the good things that He knows can help us to become better Christians and maintain a more Spirit filled life. Maintaining a thankful attitude is a good start, but is that the completion of our thanksgiving needs? The truth is that we humans are incapable of properly thanking the Almighty for anything much less everything that He has done for us.

A step closer toward properly acknowledging Him for His many kindnesses is for us to realize that He always does these things for us out of love. I don't think that it is humanly possible to fully realize how much the Good LORD truly loves each of us. Compared to Him we are only a speck in the universe; yet, he has given each of us so much. And we in turn have spoken and demonstrated so little appreciation to Him.

One of the often-overlooked things that we should be thankful for is the good testimony and godly activities of other believers. This is illustrated in the Book of Philemon.

> **"I thank my God always when I remember**
> **you in my prayers, because I hear of your**
> **love and of the faith that you have toward**
> **the LORD Jesus and all the saints,"**

> Philemon 1:4

Just saying the words is insufficient. A believer should live the kind of life that pleases the Father. Here is where all of us need to consider our motivation for doing the things that He wants us to do. Unfortunately, most, if not all, of us will only occasionally rise to the point of enlightened self-interest. We do things to please Him because we think that He will do more good things for us. This is not an expression of thanksgiving it is a feeble attempt to entice the creator of the universe into doing more good things for us. Even the most foolish person can see through this. Do you really think that the Father doesn't recognize our selfishness for what it truly is? First we should ask for His forgiveness. Then we should joyfully submit to His will and follow the leading of the Holy Spirit.

Submitting to the leading of the Holy Spirit is more complex than it sounds. First, it has to be the true intention of our hearts. If we don't mean it, we will get nowhere. We may even lose ground. Secondly, we need to immerse ourselves in the reading of His Word, His love letter to us. This should be followed by daily prayers in order to see what He sees and respond to all the nudging's of His Holy Spirit. The Holy Spirit will guide, but even good believers must consent minute by minute to be guided!

The best way a believer can respond to God's love is to purpose in his heart for God's love to flow through him to others. We are constantly in a position where we can do this. There are many people who crave even the slightest glimmer of His love and only believers are equipped to express this directly to them. With all the possibilities around us to do this we should ask ourselves one question. Why haven't we? More importantly, there will come a time when each of us will be required to give an accounting to the LORD for the miserable job we have done in representing Him in this world.

I don't expect anyone to do very much because of my prodding but each of us can choose to do better than he has! Even thou this is insufficient it is still better than no improvements at all.

If we ever met someone who adequately expressed God's love to us, we would remember them forever!

> **"If you love me, you will keep
> my commandments."**
>
> John 14:15

# CHAPTER 25

# HOW DO YOU THANK THE ALMIGHTY – PART 2

W<small>HEN A PERSON DOESN'T TRULY</small> mean the words of praise that he is speaking or singing he is being the worst kind of hypocrite. When the methods of praising the Almighty are truly the heartfelt expressions of a believer who is in fact worshiping The LORD, his praises will be fully received in the heavenly portals. The question is how does the average believer know what is an honest heart felt praise and what is not? Or can he? The average believer can't even know his own heart much less make truthful spiritual judgements concerning others.

> **"The heart is deceitful above all things, and desperately wicked: who can know it?"**
>
> Jeremiah 17:9KJV

The LORD looks at the heart of man and often sees the dark stains of unforgiven sin. When He views a clean forgiven heart in a believer who is truly appreciative of the many things the Father has done for Him it is a different picture. Praise is one way a believer can honestly express his thanks to the LORD.

> **"But you are a chosen race, a royal priesthood, a holy nation, a people for his own possession, that you may proclaim the excellences of him who called you out of darkness into his marvelous light"**
>
> I Peter 2:9

**"Yours, O LORD, is the greatest and
the power and the glory and the victory
and the majesty, for all that is in the
heavens and in the earth is yours.
Yours is the kingdom, O LORD, and
you are exalted as head above all."**

I Chronicles 29:11

NOTE 1: One of the purposes of praise is to tell others about our wonderful LORD! This is an expected extension of sincere thankfulness. A satisfied customer is still the best advertisement for anything!

Two people sing a praise song or say words of praise to the Father. They are both on an emotional high. One is hoping to placate a Holy God the other is honestly expressing his thankfulness to the Father. The difference lies in their heart. Was God's Holy Spirit promoting the praise or was it a poorly camouflaged attempt to curry favor with the Almighty? Many times, only the Father knows for sure. Some "praisers" are delusional. They think that their empty words can buy off the Almighty.

**"The heart is deceitful above all things, and
desperately wicked: who can know it. I the
LORD search the heart, I try the reins, even
to give every man according to his ways,
and according to the fruit of his doings."**

Jeremiah 17:9-10KJV

Praising the LORD can take many different forms. It can be in prayer, in statement, in song or in Holy Spirit led actions. Sometimes while praying, a hymn might come to mind. When it does I either sing it out loud or sing it in my spirit.

"Shout for joy in the LORD, O ye righteous!
Praise befits the upright. Give thanks to
the LORD with the lyre; make melody
to him with the harp of ten strings!
Sing to him a new song; play skillfully
on the strings, with a loud shouts."

Psalms 33:1-3

I believe that praise can also be expressed in the actions that one takes. I have heard some believers criticize some of the ornate beautiful churches that believers of past years have crafted. I would suggest that these structures can also be examples of true praise, if in the building of them, the builders were sincerely working as unto the LORD as an expression of praise and thanksgiving to the Eternal God that they served.

When you are truly praising the LORD don't restrict the method that you are using. Always do as the Spirit leads you. On the other hand, don't make judgements about others. If the Holy Spirit wants you to be aware of someone else's Spiritual condition He will not have any problem doing so.

**When a true believer expresses his honest heart felt praise to the Father, it is perhaps the highest form of worship that anyone on earth can experience!....**

## CHAPTER 26

# BEING ALONE WITH THE FATHER

The daily time that you set aside for your personal special prayer is when you discuss everything that you have on your mind and heart with the good LORD. It is also a time where you put forth extra effort to hear whatever He wants to communicate with you. (NOTE1: If you are concerned with a problem that you don't want to discuss with Him, then the likelihood is that it is a more serious problem than you realize! NOTE 2: He normally uses The Holy Bible illuminated by the Holy Spirit to communicate with His followers.)

Prayer time is a highpoint of your fellowship with the Master. Treasure and value each appointment. If possible this should be at the same time each day. It is best done in a quiet and private place where there are no distractions. It's just Him and you. Remember prayer is communication, you say what is on your mind and take extra care to listen carefully to whatever the GOOD LORD decides to communicate to you. NOTE 3: Be patient. Sometimes the good LORD waits until you are in a more receptive frame of mind before responding to you. Being quiet and patient can actually speed up the process.

If you choose to use a prayer list, don't just recite it and think that you have prayed for everything and everyone on it. Discuss each item with the Father. Wait for His response. His thoughts will come into your head when He is ready for you to have them. Sometimes, He will wait for a special time. When you finish one topic you may start a discussion with Him on another. After the verbal part of your prayer, meditating on the conversation is a very good next step. It will help clarify His will, and will reinforce your spiritual resolve to do His will.

The words of a good hymn or a Scripture verse can oftentimes become a vital part of your prayer. Scriptures will come to mind.

Read and meditate on the Word. Ask yourself, "Is God speaking to me." Well, who else is going to be putting Scripture verses into your mind? (NOTE 4: If you haven't studied and read the entire Bible several times, then how do you expect Him to help you recall a verse?) Meditating on His Word is a definite part of a good prayer life. When a verse containing a promise appears in your mind be careful. You could easily miss-apply it. Don't think that somehow God will automatically do something that you want just because you cited a verse. Remember Scripture is God's living Word. Treat it reverently.

During your prayer time with the LORD, you need to be aware that many of the distractions that occur during prayer and in life are directly from Satan. You may get a good idea for solving a problem that you have been working on. Just jot it down and come back to it later when you have finished praying. The phone may ring. The dog may bark. Is there some earthly thing that you deem to be more important? Hopefully not! Do whatever you can reasonably do in order to have a good visit with your heavenly Father?

Be respectful. Commune with Him about what is on your mind. Tell Him exactly what you desire. Be 100% honest. He knows your innermost thoughts. But most importantly ask that if anything that you have requested is outside of His will that he will override it. Specifically, state that you want his will to be done above everything else. His will is always better than anything that we can imagine. There is nothing better!

Oftentimes when I think I have finished praying an idea will flash through my mind. It is usually something that I think He wants me to do or it could be something that I need to discuss with Him. Sometimes the post script to a prayer is more important than the prayer itself.

Just because you have said, "amen!" doesn't mean that you have to stop praying. Just pick up where you left off and continue communicating with the Father. Saying "good-by" is not part of a prayer.

# CHAPTER 27

# FAMILY PRAYERS

It has been said many times that the family that prays together stays together. This is so true. Family prayer has been one of the traditional ways for Christian parents to introduce their children to the Father and to train them to pray and how to pray. We learn by example. It is normal for Christian families to say grace before meals. These are not the prayers I am talking about. Family prayers should be a daily gathering of the family just for prayer and Bible reading. That is it. Nothing else. It is a time of coming together as a family to discuss their concerns with the LORD of the universe. Family prayers should voice age-appropriate topics in a way that teaches the children how to pray and the importance of having a godly attitude.

Children should hear their parents pray specifically for them and their needs. Each child should hear his name mentioned in family prayer. No one should be left out. If the family pet has problems, it is appropriate to ask the good LORD for mercy and help. This is especially important for the children's spiritual development. Family prayers are a very good way of helping children to learn how to pray and how to trust the Father to provide for their needs. It also is an opportunity for children to be reminded of God's blessings and to learn to thank Him for each one of them.

Each child should be encouraged to pray out loud and to specifically ask the Good LORD about his or her needs and concerns. This is a spiritual high point in family life but it is also a good way for the parent to gauge the needs and concerns of each child. Family prayers do not replace the daily prayers of the individual and the special daily prayers of husbands and wives. These prayers are the spiritual glue that binds the couple together in a deeper level of Christian love.

The logistics of these prayers should be as consistent as possible.

If one parent has to be away at the normal prayer time care should be taken to ensure continuity. Perhaps, the one who is away could phone or Zoom in and the family could still pray together. If time zones or other factors interfere with this, the absent parent should be represented by the one who is present. Be creative. If you are hindered from doing this, consider an email prayer. Since it might confuse Google if you tried to address an email directly to the good LORD, you might opt to do this in the body of an email home. Just type the words, "Dear God" at the beginning of your prayer. If you have non prayer items to communicate you might choose to use a separate email. Pray for each other, for a safe return and include the needs of family and friends.

Everyone who can should be encouraged but not pressured to pray. Sometimes a shy child will need a little extra help. They can be asked questions about the content of a parent's prayer. For example, does the LORD want us to pray for our next-door neighbors, a sick friend, or perhaps someone the child knows that is having a hard time? NOTE 1: Gage the prayer's content so that it is appropriate for the child's maturity level. There are some concerns that a child is not able to deal with. You can always pray for someone's happiness or good health. NOTE 2: Never discount the value and effectiveness of a child's prayer. The good LORD treasures each of them.

One of the best ways of beginning a family prayer time is after reading a Bible story. (Egermeier's Bible Story Book is recommended) As the children mature deeper sections of Scriptures should be read. At some point the child should be asked to participate in the Bible readings. Hopefully, as the child grows and matures he will be able to take his turn and lead the family prayer time. Everyone should participate and have the opportunity to share in Scripture readings and prayer.

The child who experiences this in their home will find it easier to start family devotions when he or she leaves the nest and starts their own family. NOTE 3: This prayer and Bible reading time should be in addition to whatever prayers and Bible readings that you do at mealtime. Family prayer is not a replacement for individual prayer.

Some people may have a question as to the scheduling of family prayer, parents' prayers, and individual prayers. Don't worry about the sequence. If after hearing your children or spouse pray you may sense the need to pray again. Pray! There is no limit to the amount of prayers that you can offer. Ask yourself: Is there anything more important?

# CHAPTER 28

# PUBLIC PRAYERS

Public prayers are important. They normally happen when one or more people are asked to voice a prayer for a group. In public prayer, even in Churches, not everyone there will be a believer. Both weaker Christians and unbelievers need to hear and see firsthand what the good LORD can and will do in order to draw a lost and wondering sheep unto Himself. In the Bible public prayers were normally short and private prayers were normally long.

NOTE 1: Public prayers should not to be used as just another slot in a program. Prayer is the most important part of the program. The selection of who should be asked to pray is a serious matter. If possible, he or she should be asked beforehand. This gives them time for personal prayer where they can ask the LORD to forgive and to guide them. You don't want someone praying for your cause who is carrying the burden of unconfessed sins.

Unfortunately, the selection of a person to pray is often based on their elegance in verbal expression or they are asked to pray because they need to be acknowledged and have in some way earned a slot in the program. STOP! This is not the way it should be. The selection of who to pray should always be a serious spiritual task. In itself, this should be a matter of prayer.

When you call on someone give them 100% freedom. If you can't trust them, don't call on them. Their grammar and smoothness of tongue are not the most important qualifications. Their relationship with the Father is. NOTE 2: Even the best of believers will sometimes be spiritually out of kilter. Make it easy for them to decline to pray without embarrassing them.

One time at the beginning of my professional career I worked at very large plant. As part of this experience, I was asked to join a nation-wide group of professionals who did similar work. On one occasion there was a meeting of this group in a distant city, it included a meal. I rode there with another man from my office. As you could expect when we got there it began with an hour of drinking intoxicating beverages. I was offered a drink and even a coke. I declined. (It is best to not have the appearance of evil.) I knew that many people drink but I have convictions about it. I observed the event. Finally, just before the meal one drinking person asked another drinking person to say grace before we ate. He did the best that he could. I doubt that his prayer got very far. Instead, I chose to bless my meal silently. Sometimes even prayer can be offensive.

Prayer is not a form of religious poetry. It is not just another slot in a program's agenda. Early believers prayed as a group just before the Holy Spirit was given.

> **"All these with one accord were devoting
> themselves to prayer, together with
> the women and Mary the mother
> of Jesus, and his brothers."**
>
> Acts 1:14

Early believers prayed together in a home when Peter was in prison. He was delivered!

> **"When he realized this, he went to the
> house of Mary, the mother of John whose
> other name was Mark, where many were
> gathered together and were praying."**
>
> Acts 12:12

The questions that should be considered by the person who is asked to lead a group into the throne room of Almighty are: "What is the reason for the prayer? Is there a theme for the event? Is this thyme in keeping with Holy Scripture? When should you turn down a request to pray? Is there a fixed amount of time allowed for your prayer? Can you adequately pray in the circumstances and in the allotted time slot?" A casual answer is not acceptable. If in doubt decline the offer. You can still pray as you are led silently or later on in your prayer closet. Prayers should never be considered to be part of a cultural expression or just another slot in an event format.

Never forget, it is your prayer to the LORD. It is also a public forum. Let your prayers be Scripturally based. Pray the way the Spirit leads you or don't pray at all. If the person who asked you to pray tells you that you can't pray in Jesus's name; then, it is probably better to decline the invitation. However, there are ways around this. You can address your prayers to: Almighty God, The God of Abraham, Isaac, and Jacob. etc. There are lots of acceptable ways to address the Father. If you sense that they have changed their mind about asking you to pray, then just decline. There is no need to force your prayers on anyone! Anything you need to communicate to the Master can be said directly to Him, you don't need an audience. You can have the LORD's full attention.

The only time that I know of where an audience could be beneficial is when you pray a prophetic or commitment prayer asking the Father to work in specific activities. Perhaps someone with deficient faith will see your prayer answered and will grow in his or her personal faith or they might be encouraged to ask you a question that gives you an opportunity to help them.

> **"For the LORD does nothing without revealing his secret to his servants the prophets."**
>
> Amos 3:7

# CHAPTER 29

# PRONOUNCEMENTS

This section deals with expressions that can be considered prayers and similar statements that are debatable as to whether or not they are prayers. Remember prayer is communication with the Almighty. Any conversation with Him is a prayer. Anything that He tells us is His part of a prayer. Scripture mentions many of these. Some of these are: blessings, curses, vows and prophetic utterances. These should not be confused with virtuous statements, a wise man made quotation. Some are definitely not prayers but are mentioned here only to make it clear that they are not prayers. For example, virtuous statements are not prayers. I cannot see any logical reason why they should be counted as a prayer form. But that is not to say that they are valueless. Benjamin Franklin is said to have said that a "penny saved is a penny earned". A virtuous statement that promotes thrift.

A close runner up could be prophetic utterances. These are predictions about future events. They are scattered across the spectrum. At one end is the statement by a prophet of the LORD who speaks a word about the future under the full influence of the Holy Spirit. At the bottom end is a person speculating on the outcome of a horse race or a stock increasing in value.

Another pronouncement is the blessing spoken before a meal. It is a prayer where one asks the Father to bless the meal that they are about to eat. When a person sneezes and someone says "bless you" or "God bless you", it could go either way depending on their intent.

A very difficult to categorize statement is when one rebukes Satan. An example of this is when a believer rebukes Satan and commands him in Jesus' name to cease some evil activity.

> "But when the archangel Michael, contending
> with the Devil, was disputing about the
> body of Moses, he did not presume to
> pronounce a blasphemous judgement,
> but said, "The LORD rebuke you."

Jude 1:9

**One should be extremely careful about using his presumed spiritual power of attorney attaching Jesus 'name as a co-signer to any of your demands.**

If you are filled with the love that the Good LORD gives true believers you will not want anyone to be punished for ever. As a believer you have a Devine assignment to help save the lost by presenting the gospel in your life and from your mouth to the unsaved.

# CHAPTER 30

# SPECIAL PURPOSE PRAYERS - VOWS

Vows ARE A SPECIAL CATEGORY of prayers. Basically, a vow is a seriously made promise to do or not to do something with the often hope of support from the good LORD. NOTE 1: a vow is not a deal or bargain with the LORD. A vow that is performed under the leadership of the Holy Spirit carries weight with the Almighty. A vow is a very serious solemn promise that should never be made casually.

A near relative of vows are covenants. These are a special type of promise that the Good LORD makes. These are normally to a group of people. Sometimes people make agreements that they call covenants. In my opinion, covenants are more significant than vows. When the LORD makes one with a person or group of people there is often a severe penalty associated with breaking it. Scriptures have examples of people making covenants. It is my understanding that the good LORD will keep his part of a covenant regardless of whether or not the people under it agree or disagree. Since both The good LORD and people exchange communication with each other in making covenants; they can be loosely called prayers. Devine covenants are very rare.

On the other extreme there is swearing. Swearing is forbidden in Scripture (Matthew 5:33-37). One of the meanings of the word "swearing" is a solemn affirmation that something is true. i.e., swearing in court or making a special promise of loyalty as when one is entering the military. While one could play word games trying to distinguish the differences between vows, swearing and making promises they are all similar in some ways and different in others. Since the purpose is to provide spiritual help, I will not wade into defining and cataloging each word with all of the possibilities associated with them. Even if I did, no doubt, many would disagree with me. However, I will list various types of special proclamations that are acceptable and types of promises that are not acceptable.

Types of unacceptable statements that are unacceptable – Swearing

1. A special statement stating that something you are saying is true. According to Matthew 5 vs. 37KJV **"let your communication be, Yea, yea; Nay, nay: for whatsoever is more than these cometh of evil."** Don't lie. Swearing is an attempt to drag the Good LORD into confirming that you are telling the truth. This is a dangerous thing to do. If you consistently tell the truth, then your word should be sufficient. In legal matters, in the United States, you can make a statement that you affirm that you are speaking the truth.

2. Another meaning of swearing is making profane statements. A believer should not make any profane statements! Bad language is not acceptable. If bad language is the only way that you can communicate a necessary thought, then spend some time studying the dictionary.

3. Any statement that you know to be untrue. For Example: You make a statement and at the time of the statement you know that it is untrue or when you make a statement that you believe to be true and later find out that it isn't you are obligated to correct it. A close relative of this is when a person parses their words so that they camouflage a lie so well that it appears to be true. Deception is not appropriate for believers. Be Honest. In the world one might have heard the phrase, "Speak truth to power." The citers of this are proud and actually believe that they are quoting a virtuous statement. I think not! Speak the truth to everyone!

> **"...and all liars, shall have their part in the lake which burneth with fire and brimstone: which is the second death."**
>
> Revelation 21:8bKJV

The good LORD does not treat lying casually.

Types of promises that can be acceptable - vows

1. A specific promise to the LORD that you are going to do or not do something. This is a most serious statement. It is better to not make it than it is to make it and then fail. i.e., wedding vows.

**"It is better that you should not vow
than that you should vow and not pay."**

Ecclesiastes 5:5

2. A Nazarite vow. (Numbers 6:2-21) – This was a special vow of abstinence for the purpose of being a holier person who chose to do the LORD's work. The person who was a Nazarite was required to: separate himself to the LORD, separate himself from wine and strong drink, drink no vinegar made from wine or strong drink, drink any juice of grapes or eat grapes, fresh or dried. He shall eat nothing that is produced by the grapevine, not even the seeds or the skins. No razor shall touch his head. The locks of his hair shall grow long. He couldn't go near a dead body. Jesus was a Nazarite. He was also a resident of the town of Nazareth. The two are not related.

# CHAPTER 31

# BLESSINGS

Oftentimes during a ship launching ceremony, a blessing is pronounced over the ship and all who sail in her. Traditionally, Christians say a blessing before eating a meal. Hopefully, they are literally praying and not just repeating a set of words. Prayer should always be taken seriously. A blessing is a pronouncement where the one doing the blessing is in effect asking God the Father to help someone or some cause. It is practiced as an extension of one's faith. It is a spiritual request that the Father do good things for someone's betterment. Saying thank you to the Father after a blessing is very appropriate and indicates both thankfulness and faith that you trust God to take care of His children. When a person is not grateful for the many things that the Almighty is constantly doing for him he is in a very sad state and he or she definitely needs a spiritual booster shot. A blessing is in effect a request for His help. It can be specific, i.e., in some area of one's life or it can be a general request.

In I Kings chapter 3 Solomon prays for wisdom. In vs. 10-13 God expresses His acceptance of Solomon's request and gave him more than he asks for. In the next verse the LORD put a condition on His answer.

> **"And if you will walk in my ways, keeping**
> **my statutes and my commandments,**
> **as your father David walked, then**
> **I will lengthen your days."**

> I Kings 3:14

The book of Ruth contains a wonderful blessing:

**"The LORD repay you for what you have
done, and a full reward be given you by
the LORD, the God of Israel, under whose
wings you have come to take refuge!"**

Ruth 2:12

Perhaps the most familiar blessing is the one said before meals. It is a thank you blessing. In it one expresses they're thanks to the Father for providing the nourishment that those who are about to eat will receive. Often not said is the implied thought that the good LORD will keep the diners safe from any contamination that might be in the food and that the nourishment provided by it will be used to do His assignments. This is also useful reminder of why each of us is still here.

There are other types of blessings. Generally, a blessing is the expressed desire for the LORD to do good things and protect the one receiving the blessing and for them to be better enabled to do the task that He has created them to do. Be careful that in the process of making pronouncements that you don't carelessly bless an activity or cause that the good LORD has disapproved.

Another way of describing a blessing is that the one doing the blessing is verbalizing something good that the LORD wants said. Be careful when you are doing this. If possible have a Scripture to back up you're blessing and cite it. Don't be presumptuous of the Almighty.

In the Old Testament (Genesis chapter 48) there is example of a father pronouncing a special blessing over each of his children. This is a good practice to follow. You might select a special occasion for these blessings. Perhaps, you can pronounce it just before you say goodbye, when they are going on their first overnight visit or any other trip away from home. Another opportunity is when they began a new venture. A paper route, a part time job, going off to school, or their first real job. How would you have felt if you were to get a telephone call with your parents praying for you to have a successful new venture?

Another often overlooked facet of a blessing it that each of us should be a blessing to everyone that we meet. Put forth an effort so that each person that you come in contact with will in some way be better off than they were before you met them. It may be as little as a smile or a friendly word. Let each person that you come in contact with be reminded that you are here to do the will of your loving heavenly Father! NOTE 1: If you are truly trying to be a blessing it, it will be noticed! NOTE 2 Don't expect earthly acknowledgements. They are rare!

# CHAPTER 32

# CURSES

**W**ARNING! THIS CHAPTER SHOULD NOT be taken lightly or read idly out of curiosity! When curses are misused they can cause multiple very bad results to numerous people, including yourself! It is far better to ignore this topic, than to skim over it quickly. If you believe that your spiritually level is less than it should be then go directly to **chapter 33. Chapter 32's content is only for mature Christians.** Curses are mentioned numerous places in the Bible. Unless you are committed to seeking out and understanding all of the truth in God's Word, then you are better off without this information. This chapter is written only for the very few who are mature in their faith!

A curse is a spiritual pronouncement. It is in effect a type of prayer that request the LORD punish someone or something for being severely out of line with God's Word and hindering or menacing His will being done. It should not be pronounced casually. It is one of the gravest statements that a person can make. If in doubt don't. One of the consequences of pronouncing an undeserved curse on someone is that it may backfire and the curse will land on the one who wrongly pronounced it.

> **"Like a sparrow in its flitting, like a swallow in its flying, a curse that is causeless does not alight."**
>
> Proverbs 26:2

Tread carefully. Curses should be exceptionally rare and one should seriously pray about them before pronouncing them. Like a blessing the one pronouncing them is in effect attempting to say something that the good LORD wants said. This is an enormous responsibility and is not to be entered into lightly. If you can't find a Scripture that supports the curse, then you will probably be better off by not pronouncing it. Speaking of the Jews the LORD said:

**"I will bless those who bless you, and him who dishonors you I will curse, and in you all families of the earth shall be blessed."**

Genesis 12:3

**"You shall not revile God, nor curse a ruler of your people."**

Exodus 22:28

**"You shall not curse the deaf or put a stumbling block before the blind, but you shall fear your God: I am the LORD."**

Leviticus 19:14

**"How can I curse whom God has not cursed? How can I denounce whom the LORD has not denounced?"**

Numbers 23:8

**"See, I am setting before you today a blessing and a curse: the blessing, if you obey the commandments of the LORD your God, which I command you today, and the curse, if you do not obey the commandments of the LORD your God, but turn aside from the way that I am commanding you today, to go after other gods that you have not known."**

Deuteronomy 11:26-28

**"bless those who curse you, pray
for those who abuse you."**

Luke 6:28

**"Bless those who persecute you;
bless and do not curse them."**

Romans 12:14

There are two columns in the Exhaustive Concordance of the Bible that list the occurrences of the word "curse". Like it or not curses are an element in Scripture. It is good to know and understand what the Holy Bible says about every issue. To this extent I am purposefully not going any further in this topic. If you are led to study this subject further, I suggest that you first examine yourselves and determine why you are pondering this pursuit. If you believe that the Holy Spirit is leading you into this study tread softly, systematically and most of all prayerfully. Select an unabridged Concordance and carefully read every verse that includes the words: curse, cursed, or anything that seems similar. Make your motivation to study this topic a matter of serious prayer. May you never be in a situation where you sincerely believe that pronouncing a curse is appropriate!

NOTE 1: A curse does not have to have the word "curse" in it. See Nehemiah 4:4-5. Here a curse was pronounced in a prayer to punish the people who were seriously hindering God's will from being done. In the New Testament Paul pronounced a curse. NOTE 2: The conditions surrounding the curse. He was led by the Holy Spirit. See Acts 13: 6-12. This action resulted in someone being saved.

# CHAPTER 33

# INTERCESSORY PRAYERS

> "First of all, then, I urge that supplications,
> prayers, intercessions, and thanksgivings
> be made for all people, for kings and
> all who are in high positions, that we
> may lead a peaceful and quite life,
> godly and dignified in every way."
>
> I Timothy 2:1-2

> "praying at all times in the Spirit, with
> all prayer and supplication. To that end
> keep alert with all perseverance, making
> supplication for all the saints,"
>
> Ephesians 6:18

BEING AN ENGINEER, I AM always curious about how things work. This holds true even in spiritual matters. Scripture tells us that:

> "The effectual fervent prayer of a
> righteous man availeth much."
>
> James 5:16b KJV

God does do good things as a result of His people praying for their concerns. If He were to choose to do something just because He chose to do it without any communications to us, it would be more likely that many people would have a difficult time recognizing what He did. Whatever the mechanism or reasoning is, the Father has chosen to do various things just because one or some of His followers asked for His help. I doubt that we will understand the total prayer process and what really happens as a result of prayer until He personally explains it to us. It should be sufficient for us to know that God often choses to do awesome things in response to a believer's sincere prayers.

This poses another question. Why can't a good believer just pray by himself for his own needs and let that prayer be the only one that needs to be prayed? The reason is simple. Any prayer that the good LORD answers tends to build the faith of the one who asked for His help. When many people pray for the LORD to do something the blessing, faith, and growth potentials are magnified. The most obvious blessing from an answered prayer is a strengthening of one's faith!

There are also times when the LORD will not hear one person's prayers and it is necessary for a more devout person to pray for him. For example, Job was asked to pray for his friends in (Job 42:7-9).

Another aspect of this relates to the content of James 5:16b KJV, **"The effectual fervent prayer of a righteous man availeth much."** The more people praying for the same purpose the more likely it is that among them are a few more righteous people. God does do special things because righteous people ask Him for help. NOTE 1: A truly righteous person will always want the LORD's will to be done above everything else. Some people mistakenly think that because a large number of people are asking for the same thing that the Good LORD is somehow more obligated to answer their request. You can't gang up against the Almighty and expect to get you own way!

One of the functions of Intercessory prayer is that we are empowered to help others by bearing some of their burdens. If we pray for them the way we are expected to, then we will not only be empathetic but by our prayers we will be carrying some of their spiritual burden. When someone else is praying for us, our burdens are lighter and much more bearable.

**"Bear one another's burdens, and
so fulfill the law of Christ."**

Galatians 6:2

The good LORD often impresses certain believers to pray for a specific need. Even though among them there may be some with a weaker faith who don't expect the LORD to do anything. The Lord may still answer their prayers. In doing so the faith of even the weakest one who prayed can be strengthened. Everyone wins when their faith in the LORD is strengthened!

The LORD not only answers our prayers, but His Holy Spirit prompts us when to pray and what to pray about. God wants to do many good things for believers and He wants them to participate in the process. One of the chief ways that any believer can participate with the Father in His wonderful works is through intercessory prayer. Believers are instructed to pray for the needs of others. This should bring much joy to the believer in that he can participate in some of God's activities. ..... It does!

In intercessory prayer the Holy Spirit moves a believer to pray for someone's need or condition. The believer who is sensitive to and obedient to the wooing's of God's Spirit will pray for others. As a result, and in God's own way and for His own reasons, He does wonderful things for that person. God likes to answer prayers. He does it in His perfect timing and in the way that best accomplishes His will. The believer on the other hand has the privilege of working together with the Almighty. This is a very high level of Devine fellowship.

Intercessory prayer is a wonderful responsibility but just like everything else there are those who get the wrong idea about it. First of all, the person who is doing the praying is not causing the actions that the LORD takes. They are only making a request out of Christian love for someone else. NOTE 2: even though believers are not causing something to happen it could be that if they fail to pray, the wonderful thing that the good LORD has chosen to do may get delayed. Perhaps this delay will last until another believer choses to pray in obedience for that need. God does everything His way, in His optimum timing, and for whatever reasons that He chooses. We humans do not have a controlling factor in this process.

At our best we can only express our God-given love for someone else to the Master.

Intercessory Prayers are appropriate for a believer to pray for another person's benefit. An example for this is found in III John. This can also be considered a blessing.

> **"Beloved, I pray that all may go well with you and that you may be in good health, as it goes well with your soul."**
>
> III John 1:2

The believer's part is simple: he is to confess his sins to the Father, ask for forgiveness, follow the wooing's of God's Holy Spirit, and to pray the way that he is led to pray. That is it. We humans are not miracle producers. At our very best we are just voices who can bring the needs of others into the throne room of our loving Almighty God. Some are more effective at this than others.

A good example of intercessory prayer is found in Acts chapter 12. Here Simon Peter is put in prison. Fearing that he would be killed, as James was, the believers gathered and prayed. There was nothing else they could do.

It would be easy to speculate that some probably asked themselves, "Who is next?" The LORD miraculously broke Peter out of jail. Peter was then led to the home where they were praying. When he got there, he knocked on the door. Rhoda went to the door and opened it. When she opened the door and recognized Peter she was so awe struck that she closed the door. Then she went and told the others. When they came to the door they rejoiced at what the LORD had done. These early believers didn't know what the LORD would do as a result of their prayers, but they knew that He loved them and were led to pray for the needs of a fellow believer that they dearly loved. They had no other option!

Intercessory prayer is not limited to just praying for a few special people. The list is endless. The general charge is to pray for any need that the Holy Spirit places on your heart. For example, you can pray for a lost person to be saved, a sick person to be healed, for discord between two believers to be turns into friendship, for a person without a job to get employed, for a person who is traveling you can request journeying mercies etc. The key is to always pray for God's will to be done. Don't worry about how the good LORD is going to work things out. Just trust Him to do the things that he has chosen to do. His response is far better than anything that we can imagine. NOTE 3: Don't fall into the trap of telling the Almighty, All Knowing Creator of the Universe how He needs to help out in a given situation. Just ask Him to do the best thing that He can. He is a lot smarter and many times more powerful than we can imagine. Trust Him, He loves each of us very much! NOTA BENE (Note well) **One of His main concerns for us is our holiness!**

# CHAPTER 34

# COMMITMENT PRAYERS

Commitment prayers are one of the most powerful prayers a believer can pray for himself, others, or for some good ongoing or upcoming purpose. I pray them often and I have consistently received very good outcomes. The Good LORD answers His way and I get the benefits. Many times, His actions are so unpredictable that I could not have imagined them as valid possibilities.

Even good believers often overlook a most obvious fact. The good LORD is immeasurably times smarter than we could ever imagine. Yet in our fragile humanity we often end up trying to tell Him how to do something that we want done or that we feel that He needs to act upon.

For example: We become aware of something in our environment and see the possibility of different things happening. Some of these are bad. In our minds we can imagine some actions of how these bad events can be changed for the betterment of all concerned. We quickly realize that in our own strength and knowledge that we cannot cause any of the good solutions by ourselves. Many times, they are clearly humanely impossible. About this time, we began to think that our Heavenly Father can do the very things that we think will solve the problem and we ask him to help out. This is where most of us go wrong. We decide how the problem should be handled and assign our supernatural cure to the Almighty. **THIS IS A HUGE MISTAKE!** Both spiritually and logically. The best thing that a true believer can do is to commit the entire outcome to the Good LORD. In His wisdom He will see a solution that we could never imagine. He can work things out far better than we could even dream. His way is always the best outcome for any problem. Meditate on these points.

1. God has all knowledge, past present, and future.
2. God is all powerful.
3. God loves each of us very much and wants the very best for all of us.
4. He wants our faith in Him to increase.
5. He wants each of us to be holy!

**Now, isn't it really dumb for us to tell Him, The Creator of the Universe how He should handle a bad situation. That is why committing the outcome to Him and trusting Him to select the method or action is very important. Sometimes the bad result of an event is a part of His correction process. For some conditions a severe correction is necessary in order to guide a wondering sheep back to the Shepard! ....**

The best prayers are prayed in agreement with Holy Scriptures and express trust in the good judgement of the all-Knowing God. The most effective and powerful prayer a person can pray is for His Will to be done. There is nothing better than God's will! The commitment prayer is one of these prayers. Here the believer brings a problem or concern to the Father and commits it to His good judgement and ask for His will to be done. When prayed sincerely and honestly by a forgiven believer, it is an always answered prayer. What is your prayer "batting average"?

Stop and think for a moment. What do you think Moses thought the LORD would do when he had the Red Sea on one side and Pharos army coming toward them on the other side?

When you ask for God's will to be done, it is. His answer is not always what you expected or even wanted, but it is the best possible outcome. If you really believe that God is many times smarter than you are, that He knows the future, that he loves you more than anyone else, and that he desires only the very best for you, then why can't you trust Him to select the solution that He deems to be the best? It is always a matter of trust. Do you really trust God! Faith deficiencies are fertilized by sin. Satan consistently creates doubt.

God's answer may not be the one you thought you needed or wanted because the Good LORD places our holiness far above our personal desires. He knows and does what is best? Trust Him!

> **"Watch and pray that you may not**
> **enter into temptation. The spirit indeed**
> **is willing, but the flesh is weak."**
>
> Matthew 26:41

Commitment prayers are usually short and simple. As a believer, who is in good standing with the Master, it is best when you choose to rely upon the good judgement and watchful eye of the LORD. For example, you are going on a short trip to a nearby city. Your thoughts may turn to an accident or a carjacking that recently occurred. As a result, you ask the Father to watch over you and you commit the trip and the purpose of the trip into His good care. When you get home you should thank Him for His watch care over you. In another case you may be taking on another challenge and you may not know how to handle it. You pray a prayer of commitment to the Father and He governs events so that His will is accomplished.

Eventually, an unbelieving friend might enquire about how it was possible that you got the results you got. This is a witnessing opportunity and you should take full advantage of it by giving the good LORD total credit for the victory. The only possible credit that you might try to claim is that you had the good sense to commit it to the good LORD. When you take the credit for the LORD's works there is a severe penalty. NOTE 1: He also gave you the good sense to call on Him. So, in all honesty you can't even take credit for that.

"Commit thy way unto the LORD; trust also in him; and He shall bring it to pass."

Psalms 37:5KJV

"Commit thy works unto the LORD, and thy thoughts shall be established."

Proverbs 16:3KJV

# CHAPTER 35

# PRAYERS FOR GUIDANCE

LIFE IS FILLED WITH DECISIONS. The requirement to make some decisions are forced upon us. Sometimes there are options. Many times, the best option is unknown. Sometimes the options page is blank. There are times when you need to be proactive, but in which direction? You wake up in the morning and ask yourself," What am I going to do today?" Life consists of many decisions. For each decision there are consequences. Some are good and some are bad. Many are mixtures. Even when you know what God's will is in an important matter, it is still very important to seek His path in order to arrive where He wants you to be.

The way you do His will is important. In some, if not all, cases the path that He wants you to follow may be more important than the intended destination. Many decisions are a mixture of plusses and minuses. Do you take the medicine that tastes bad in order to get well? How do you make your selections? Do you ask and trust the good, all knowing Father for His directions?

Casting aside all other methods, one method stands far above the nearest second best. As a believer you can get the best possible advice and guidance for any question or problem. You can personally ask your Heavenly Father," What do you want me to do?" His directions are the best possible choice because:

1. He knows everything, including the future.
2. He loves you very much and wants the best for you.
3. He custom designed you and has a unique plan for your life.
4. When you are striving toward the direction that he has selected for you, he goes before you and prepares the way. (His path shapes you toward becoming Holy!)
5. His wide-ranging directions are already written for you in The Holy Bible.

What more could one ask for? Well suppose you have asked and you don't see anything happening. NOTE 1: His general directions are written down in the Scriptures. When we are not following them, why should we expect Him to give us special detailed instructions?

I followed the best directions I had, and still nothing happened! Now, what do I do? A very valid question. Today, we want everything instantly. We often feel that we can't wait. One of our problems is that we lack patience. Patience helps us develop our meditation and prayer skills, which are severely lacking in our age of prosperity and instant everything.

There are also other concerns associated with doing God's will. What we need to do first is to determine what is wrong. Is it a personal shortcoming? Is someone else in rebellion? Are we trying to go against God's will?

We all have problems accurately determining God's will and we need to go about it in a logical spiritual manner. In technical terms this is similar to troubleshooting an automotive problem. I believe the spiritual process is similar. First establish if your prayers got through to the Master. To do this you must be honest with yourself. Am I in a state of spiritual rebellion? Do I really want Gods will? If you don't truly want God's will, then you are, without exception, in rebellion. (Some rebellions are milder than others.) There is only one way for anyone to be victorious. You need to confess your sins to the Father and ask for His forgiveness and then ask for and welcome His directions. If you meant what you have just prayed; then, wait patiently with your eyes, ears, and spiritual reception on and at full volume. NOTE 2: A key part of waiting is purposeful Bible study. Most likely His answer is in the Word! You will get your answer when and how the good LORD decides to give it to you. Remember, prayer is a two-way conversation. We have one mouth and two ears. The effort we put into listening is proportional to the amount of faith that we have. Clear answers to prayer build more faith.

Some people use the example of a boat when discussing the process of seeking God's guidance. A boat that is standing still is difficult to steer. However, when a boat is moving it can be guided more easily. This illustration has both a positive and a negative aspect. There are times when the best thing anyone can do is wait. Other times it is best to be moving or making preparations for the next possibility. Ask the Father to help you do the things that He currently wants you to do. By doing these things you will be in a better position to discern His will for tomorrow. When you can't sense the direction that the good LORD wants you to take, pray. Should you be in a position where you must make a decision that you can't delay then use the brain that the LORD gave you. Do the best that you can. Be open to His course correction process. If you sincerely want to be in His will, He will help you to get there. You might not know until the very last second which choice to make. There may even be a few rare circumstances where any choice you make is fine. Don't count on it. Seeking God's will and His directions is a never-ending task.

**"In all thy ways acknowledge him,
and he shall direct thy paths."**

Proverbs 3:6 KJV

There are some basic questions that you should ask yourself.

1. Am I 100% sure that the path that I have selected is the path that the good LORD wants me to be on?
2. Why am I that sure?
3. What are the choices that I have the ability to make?
4. Has the Holy Spirit placed a verse of Scripture in my mind?
5. Am I willing to change my plans, attitude, direction, etc.?
6. Am I being driven by something that my old sin nature wants?
7. Can I discern that the Lord's will is different from the path that I am now on?
8. What is the next step that I can take in the path of God's will?

9.  Have I searched the Scriptures for guidance?
10. Have I claimed God's promises for this endeavor?
11. Why am I waiting?
12. Am I expecting a sign before I proceed? (Signs were promised to the Jews. If you are not Jewish, you may not receive a sign.) There is a difference between a sign and a confirmation.
13. What is Satan doing now?
14. **Remember! Nothing is more important than God's will!**

# CHAPTER 36

# HOW DO I RECEIVE HIS ANSWER?

You HAVE BROUGHT A PROBLEM or concern to the Good LORD. You have asked for His guidance. You have committed the outcome to Him. Well, how can you know what He wants to tell or show you? What is His response to your prayer? How do you know that a sudden incoming thought is His answer?

These are valid questions. You probably will not like my answer. They are spiritually discerned. God's Spirit communicates His answers to you. **<u>It is all about being sensitive to the Holy Spirit!</u>** The closer you are to Him the clearer the answer will be. There are exceptions! Sometimes He will use another human being to voice His instructions to you. **BUT** you still have to discern, if it is from His Spirit or a counterfeit message from Satan! The good LORD does things His way and in His timing. The way that you receive His answer is also part of the answer.

## Answers to prayers

## How does God answer prayers?

Let's assume that as a believer you have sincerely and correctly asked the Father to lead you in the path toward doing exactly what He wants you to do. As far as you can determine you did everything just right. The question still remains. How do you receive God's answer? Secondly, how do you know that the answer you received is the one that the good LORD sent you? Because God speaks in many ways, believers have to be constantly alert for incoming communications from the Master.

Many times, Satan sends counterfeit messages to God's people. Sometimes Satan's messages may seem on the surface to be an answer from the Almighty. (Satan is sly. He may even communicate an answer that is God's second or third best.) The believer needs to be able to detect and squelch the false signals that the evil one is constantly sending Him. The truth is that without the influence of the Holy Spirit none of us can correctly discern God's will.

Without any doubt the best way of hearing God's instructions is to be reading His Word with a mindset that is focused on determining what the Good LORD is saying to you through the Word. A word of caution, don't look for short cuts. Use the method of Bible reading and prayer that the Good LORD leads you to use for the matter that you are seeking help on. NOTE 1: He may choose to give you guidance on something else you need to know or do before He leads you forward in your present decision path. His priorities are often different from ours. He could use this occasion to teach you something new that you might need several years from now.

> **NOTE: A believer who carefully studies God's word each day and has read through the entire Bible several times can better and more quickly discern the messages from the Holy Spirit with considerable less effort! If you haven't studied the Bible, then how do you expect Him to help you recall a verse that you haven't read?**

> **"Ask, and it shall be given you; seek, and you shall find; knock, and it shall be opened unto you: For everyone that asketh receiveth; and he that seeketh findeth; and to him that knocketh it shall be opened."**

> Matthew 7:7-8 KJV

The Father is aware of your spiritual reception problems. He can slow down or speed up the communication link. He can speak Louder. When He doesn't answer instantly, He has a reason for the delay! Focus on the importance of you doing His will, He always does His part.

Sometimes the LORD will choose to use one of His pastors or one of His Sunday school teachers who might seem get off subject and mention something that He wants you to hear. When He does, His answer will be ever so apparent. Even when it is obvious and clear what His will is, it is easy to still feel uncertain. You may ask Him to confirm an answer as long as you are not trying to avoid or delay doing His will (See **Judges 6:36-40** and **II Samuel 7:18-29**). In your heart, doing His will needs to be the predominate factor. It is the believer's only purpose for still being here on earth!

Remember it is not His will for you to personally do every good thing that presents itself to you. Some of these things are reserved for others to do. On the other hand, someone who is better qualified may be shirking their responsibilities. The Good LORD may want you to do what they should have been doing and haven't.

He may have a stranger communicate some part of His will to you. Other times He may have selected you to say something to a stranger. When it is His will, He will highlight it in a sufficient manner in your heart. Just trust Him!

An often overlooked fact, Satan is a counterfeiter He tries to copy the things that the LORD does and slants them in his direction. Temptation is one of these things. Satan has observed how God communicates His will to people. Satan tries to use a similar process to lure people into deeper layers of sin. We have all sinned. We have all been there. It should be obvious to us the allurement process that Satan has used successfully on us. He starts with a little bit of evil that we don't think is so bad and gradually ratchets it up to full blown iniquity. This in some ways mirrors the process that the Good LORD uses to guide His followers into a more righteous life. The Good LORD plants a seed in our minds and the Holy Spirit builds on it. This works best when we are daily nourishing our new nature with His Word.

The free will aspect begins when we decide which of our two

natures we are going to feed. Whatever is nourished the most tends to flourish and grow. By the time it matures most of the decision to do or not to do an action is essentially made. Often times the LORD's answer is just wait until I am ready to tell you. This could be an essential step in His will for your life. He may be building your patience, something that He knows that you will need many times when you are doing what He created you to do. To some degree we can choose which stimulus enters our head. Some inputs we can't eliminate. Free will can work either way. We always have choices. NOTA BENE (Latin for note well). It has been said in a worldly context that the paralysis of analysis will stop any project. Dr. Kenneth F. McKinley of LeTourneau University used to say that you can't keep a bird from flying over your head but you can keep him from making a nest in your hair.

You should never fear that the Good LORD might be unable to lead you in the path that you needed to travel. Sin is always the problem. Jesus is always the answer.

# CHAPTER 37

# BUT IT IS NOT THE ANSWER I WANTED

You PRAYED. GOD ANSWERED, AND you don't like His answer. Now what do you do? That is between you and the Almighty. One of you is wrong. It is not Him! If this is the case, without a doubt, you are in some level of rebellion and you need to quickly and respectfully seek His forgiveness. First, I am not asking you to begrudgingly accept God's will. Somehow you have gotten off the narrow path and have in some way nurtured a rebellious spirit. You didn't do it all by yourself. Satan was in there doing everything that He could to derail you from doing and being in the center of God's will. There are no other possibilities, you are in some level of rebellion and you sincerely and prayerfully need to seek the LORD's forgiveness and guidance to get back onto His selected path. Nothing else can correct this condition.

Now, let's take a few deep breaths and relax for a few minutes. Not everyone who hasn't instantly seen or hasn't liked the results of their prayers is grossly backslidden. Some are! There are other possibilities that most of us have overlooked. One of the simplest is that we haven't reached out and fully grasped the answer that the good LORD has provided. It could be right under our noses and we didn't see it because we expected it to arrive in a large well wrapped package with our name on the tag.

Another often overlooked possibility is that we haven't asked the Father how He wanted us to use the answer that he provided. The good LORD does things with His overall purpose in mind. It all goes back to His perfect will being done! Once we have accepted the challenge to do His will, we can in good conscious ask Him how we are to use and respond to the answers that he has provided for us.

When we have exhausted all other possibilities, we should meditate on the one that most people choose to overlook. We need to face the music and acknowledge that we have asked for something that at least now is spiritually out of reach. Our current spiritual need should be for us to pray and ask for forgiveness and for the Holy Spirit to guide us into the condition that the Father wants us to be in. We have all been there at one time or another!

Should He want you to do something urgently, don't worry. He can do whatever is necessary to guide you back into His will. (Which do you prefer: His gentle shepherding or His spiritual dynamite? Stubbornness has consequences.)

Before we get all disheveled, we need to consider some of the other real possibilities. Could it be that the answer that we received is one notch closer to a future step in God's will? A valid possibility is that sometimes a small action is part of an overall process and we have just gotten out of step with His ideal path. Sometimes even a good believer will desire something good so much that he will lose his focus on how the LORD wants His will to be accomplished. The path that He wants you to follow toward doing or receiving something is a vital part of His will. This path is also part of His long term will for your life. Do you trust Him?

For example: In the Scriptures it tells us about a person who was invited to a party (**Luke 14:8-11**). It was a large gathering. Upon entering the guest was led to an unimportant seat. Later, when the host arrived, he led the guest to a much better seat. Everyone now knew the importance of the guest. The lesser seat turned out to be a step in the right direction.

Regardless of what we wished for, regardless of what we asked for, regardless of how we have expected God's will to unfold, we are all still human and we are always the one who is deficient. Don't expect the Almighty Creator to change His plans in any way in order to better accommodate us. Never under estimate the wiles of the Devil. He is a distorter and counterfeiter of everything that the good LORD does. Keep in mind that you are a child of the King and He has wonderful plans for you. Satan's interferences can be defeated.

The old adage about when you are handed a bunch of lemons

make lemonade is true in the spiritual world. If you don't see His purpose in what you have been handed, ask the GOOD LORD for wisdom and guidance. When He sees that you are ready to do His will, He will help you discern what you need to know and do. If other things are necessary, you can count on Him to provide whatever is needed for it to be done. A major slice of this rests upon us having the attitude that he wants us to have in order for us to properly carry out His plan.

Let's face it, on a day-to-day basis we may think that we are between assignments. It is also possible that our daily walk and our attitude could be the most important part of God's will for us. After all. That is how we spend the most time. ....

If we are having communication problems, then we need to have an attitude that demonstrates the work of the Holy Spirit living in us. He may want us to reflect His light to someone else that has similar problems. To do His will successfully, our attitude needs to project a good relationship with the Father.

We are all down here on temporary assignment. Our permanent residence is with Him in Heaven. Those who follow His directions devoutly tend to get more and better upgrades. Sometimes when we do a good job at one assignment, He in turn, may give us a harder assignment that others might have difficulty doing.

# CHAPTER 38

# PRAYERS FOR FORGIVENESS

Many of us would like to skip this chapter. The rest of us may try to convenience ourselves that we are up-to-date in asking the Almighty for His forgiveness. As long as we are here on earth there is always something that we should be asking the LORD to forgive us for doing or thinking. The sin of "pride" is a good universal starting point. (NOTE 1: there is a difference between pride and self-esteem. Having an accurate sense of who you are in God's eyes is essential to self-esteem. Whereas pride is a false belief that you are somehow more deserving and better than your peers.). Having doubts related to God's Word or a lack of faith in Him is a close runner-up.

Unfortunately, in order for some people to seek forgiveness they must first feel the chastisement of the Good LORD. When one of His children is severely out of step with the Father, He reminds him of his need to repent. Rebellion and stubbornness are costly. The prophet Jeremiah (see Lamentations chapter 5) gives us some ideas of how far backslidden God's people were. In this case a severe correction was needed.

It is God's desire for each believer to be holy. He does whatever is necessary in order for us to seek a closer relationship with Him. Think about a small child that tends to run out into a busy street. A loving parent will disincline and restrain the child sufficiently in order to keep him safe. The Father always acts out of love. Pride is expensive and can cause spiritual pain!

On the other hand, forgiveness is a matter of being honest with both the LORD, ourselves and the ones that we have harmed. We are guilty and if we truly mean that we regret sinning, then we need to name the sin and honestly confess it. (NOTE 2: A good rule to follow is that sins committed in private should be acknowledged privately whereas sins that have been committed publicly should be acknowledged publicly.) **When we sincerely pray for forgiveness it is an always instantly answered prayer in the affirmative**. The problem for many people is that they don't follow up on their forgiveness prayers. Normally, after praying for forgiveness another temptation pops up and we allow it to take its place. Pride can easily slip back in. The recently forgiven can easily start thinking of themselves as being better than their associates since they are now forgiven.

The goodness in the act of forgiveness always belongs to the one who does the forgiving. The forgiven gets to start things over again with a clean slate. And it is some cases, again, and again and again. It almost seems like a losing situation. However, even though victory over sins is realistically possible only with the help of the Holy Spirit. It, on the other hand, is not possible for anyone to completely stop sinning as long as he or she is on planet earth. That is why we are always needing to keep asking for His forgiveness.

Asking for forgiveness does not give the repentant immunity toward not sinning. It should however help one to become more sensitive to the voice of the Holy Spirit and becoming more skilled at recognizing and resisting upcoming temptations by obeying the Holy Spirit. If you are tempted to rob a bank, then don't drive by it!

Any believer who continuously chooses to follow the LORD's leading can be consistently victorious. The holy life that the Father desires for each of us to have is obtainable. NOTE 3: It is only possible through His spiritual strength that we can appropriate spiritual victories as we continue to do the LORD's will. Part of this is to promptly and earnestly request His forgiveness whenever we sin. Over a period of time the severity of our sins and the frequency of their occurrences should be constantly decreasing.

Believers should always be choosing for His will to be done. The holy life can only be complete when we arrive in heaven. Until then we need to quickly ask for forgiveness as often as His Spirit convicts us of sinning. Unfortunately, there are some who desperately need to ask for forgiveness and are so successfully besieged by Satan and are so absorbed in their sins that they don't consider asking the LORD for His forgiveness. Some may have been deceived into thinking that their deeds and their consequences will somehow fade away over time even if they don't ask for forgiveness. They misinterpret reality. What actually happens is that with repeated sinning their conscious becomes more calloused over time. This is a very bad dangerous condition! It will be corrected if the person is in fact a believer!

> **"As many as I love, I rebuke and chasten:
> be zealous therefore, and repent."**
>
> Revelation 3:19 KJV

**(NOTE 4: If He doesn't correct you when you have Sinned, then you are not one of His children!)**

There is not a shortage of forgiveness' from the LORD. That is one of the many things that He offers abundantly to all of those who sincerely ask, as long as they are still alive, after that it is TOO LATE!!!

When a person has received the LORD's forgiveness, he is ready to continue the forgiveness process. You mean there is more. Yes, there is. Oftentimes, the next step is to ask a fellow human for their forgiveness of the wrongdoing that you have committed against them. This is prompted by the Holy Spirit.

Asking for human forgiveness often requires a substantial amount of moral courage. To get the necessary courage one needs to ask the Father for His help. Even with His help this can be a difficult thing to do. It is made more difficult by Satan and the forces of darkness that he has mustered against you.

Restitution is the next step in the forgiveness process. Here we do our best to restore or make up for the sin that we have committed. If we stole or wrongly appropriated something we need to restore the owner's property. If we have said something that is hurtful and untrue about someone we need to correct it as best we can. (These are often very difficult things to do but never-the-less they are vitally necessary.) ….

After receiving forgiveness from the person, we have sinned against, it is now necessary to ask the good LORD for his help in resisting future temptations. You are forgiven but the process is not yet complete. The believer is now in a position where he should minute by minute claim the LORD's help in resisting the next onslaught of the craftily temptations that Satan will surely bring his way. (NOTE 5: Satan doesn't give up. He may choose to not be obvious for a short period of time in order to trick you into thinking that you have conquered a sin.)

> **"No temptation has overtaken you that**
> **is not common to man. God is faithful,**
> **and he will not let you be tempted beyond**
> **your ability, but with the temptation**
> **he will also provide the way of escape,**
> **that you may be able to endure it."**
>
> I Corinthians 10:13

Each of these steps involve basic prayer functions. It is humanly impossible to correctly go through this process without following up continuously with the Good LORD! There are lots of forgiveness prayer possibilities. How strong is your desire to be in the best possible relationship with the Almighty?

NOTE 6: When a believer has sincerely prayed one forgiveness prayer for a given act of sinning he is 100% forgiven of the sin or sins that he has included in the prayer. The follow-up items are usually things that the good LORD may ask you to do! He always knows what is best!

NOTE 7: Forgiveness does not automatically eliminate all the earthly consequences of the sin.

NOTE 8: It is imperative to do the follow up assignments that are prompted by the Holy Spirit. When He is ignored it is a very serious SIN. It could result in the Spirit leaving you alone for a time. This is perhaps the most spiritually dangerous thing that could happen to a believer.

# "Quench not the Spirit."

I Thessalonians 5:19KJV

## CHAPTER 39

# PRAYER PROMISES

W̲ʜᴀᴛ ɪꜱ ᴀ ᴘʀᴀʏᴇʀ ᴘʀᴏᴍɪꜱᴇ? A prayer promise is not a legally binding contract between a believer and the Almighty. But there are similarities. It is a clear invitation from God to believers to request His Devine help in something that concerns them. Normally there are stipulations and conditions that must be met. The most imperative condition is that the request must be in God's will?

NOTE 1: All humans have many needs and desires. The Father also has many things that He wants them to do. A prayer promise is an open invitation for a believer to address his specific and often heart felt desires and needs to the only one who can perfectly satisfy them. He always has a much better response than we could dream up. Trust the good LORD and always ask for his will to be done for each perceived need.

> **"He shall call upon me, and I will answer him: I will be with him in trouble; I will deliver him and honour him."**
>
> Psalms 91:15KJV

> **"Before they call I will answer; while they are yet speaking I will hear."**
>
> Isaiah 65:24

> **"And I tell you, ask, and it will be given to you; seek, and you will find; knock, and it will be opened to you. For everyone who ask receives, and the one who seeks finds, and to the one who knocks it will be opened."**
>
> "Luke 11:9-10

> "If you abide in me, and my words abide
> in you, ask whatever you wish, and it
> will be done for you. By this my Father
> is glorified, that you bear much fruit
> and so prove to be my disciples."

John 15:7-8

> "If my people who are called by my name
> humble themselves, and pray and seek
> my face and turn from their wicked ways,
> then I will hear from heaven and will
> forgive their sin and heal their land."

II Chronicles 7:14

> "Therefore I tell you, whatever you
> ask in prayer, believe that you have
> received it, and it will be yours."

Mark 11:24

Okay, okay there are lots and lots of wonderful promises in the Bible. I too have prayed many prayers based on them. But how do you think the GOOD LORD responded to our promise-claiming prayers? We don't always know. Did we make a request that is outside of God's will? What did we really expect to happen? Is my faith deficient? There is only one perfect request: That His will is done.

Prayer promises are one way the Good LORD uses to remind us of some of the many things that He does and that He is willing to do for his children. Most of them describe actions that only the LORD can do. Most if not all of them are conditional. That is, we need to meet the requirements that are contained in the verse and in many other relevant verses in the Word. NOTE 2: There are some unique needs that some believers may have that are not easily found in Scripture. Just because you can't find a verse that describes your exact perceived need doesn't mean that it is not included in a promise that you haven't completely studied or understood.

The point is that when we are led to believe that we need the Good LORD's help: we should ask Him for it. Perhaps the need or desire is so vaguely defined that we can't easily put it into words. A believer who is up to date in his requests for forgiveness can legitimately ask for God's help and when necessary His intervention.

Imagine an unbeliever who is viewing one of the LORD's works in you and he is being acted upon by the Holy Spirit. He will likely end up awed by what the Good LORD does. The Holy Spirit may even use those actions to convict the human subject of your prayers of his sins and lead him into to becoming a new believer! Never underestimate what the Good LORD will to do as the result of the sincere honest prayers of a forgiven believer. He is not limited by our imaginations.

Prayer is critical in every step in the spiritual growth process. No one can grow spiritually all by himself!

# CHAPTER 40

# LESSONS FROM PRAYERS THAT ARE RECORDED IN SCRIPTURE

1.  Abraham prays for his nephew Lot who moved to Sodom in **Genesis 18:23-33** - When our friends and relatives do something we know is wrong we should pray for them to repent and ask the good LORD for His mercy.

2.  Jacob prayed at Peniel see **Genesis 32:24-30** – Here prayer is compared to a wrestling match. Believers will always be struggling spiritually toward doing and accepting God's will. The battle is between our old nature and our new nature. We only win when the LORD wins! Doing God's will is seldom the easiest path.

3.  David wanted to build the temple but because of his sin he was told that he couldn't build it. See **II Samuel 7:4-29** - Most believers have some degree of spiritual aspiration. Remember some things are reserved for others to do. Don't worry about the other things. Just do the part that the Good LORD has assigned to you. And do your part at the best level that you can with a godly attitude, always depending on the Holy Spirit to help and guide you. No more is necessary.

4.  Solomon's prayer dedicating the Temple as recorded in **I Kings 8:22-54**.

    a.  He acknowledged who God is.
    b.  He acknowledged that God loves His people.
    c.  He asked God to confirm His promises.
    d.  He asked God to hear him.

    e.  He asked God to answer their prayers.

    f.  He asked God to forgive His people.

    g.  He asked God to vindicate the righteous.

    h.  He acknowledged the consequences of sin.

    i.  He asked God for guidance.

    j.  He asked God to take care of His people.

    k.  He asked that everyone learn about God.

    l.  He asked for victory in life's battles.

5.  Elijah prayed at Carmel **I Kings 18:36-39** – Elijah acknowledged that He belonged to God. He requested that God answer him so that others would get to know the LORD. God responded with fire from heaven.

6.  Hezekiah prayed for defense at the invasion of Sennacherib **II Kings 19:15-19** - Save us (a help prayer), that everyone would know the LORD. A short prayer, God's response to his prayer is recorded in the next 13 verses!

7.  Jabez prayed in **I Chronicles 4:10** – He asked for a blessing, that God would be with him and he asked for protection. God answered his prayer.

8.  David's prayer in **I Chronicles 17:16-27** for God to preserve his family – He acknowledged God's help in his life. He praised God, and requested blessings for his people so that they would know about God forever and recognize His blessings.

9.  Nehemiah's prayer in **Nehemiah 1:4-11** is a prayer for national forgiveness and the privilege of working in God's will

10.  Hezekiah prayed for healing in **Isaiah 38:3-6** – He asked God to remember his walk. God responded by adding fifteen years to his life.

11. Ezra prayed concerning the sins of Israel **Ezekiel 9:8** – He Prayed for God to be merciful to Israel. Asking the LORD for mercy is always an appropriate prayer. He acknowledged that God is in control of everything and that He loves each of us. It also indicated that His people are dependent upon Him.

12. Daniel prayed for the captive Jews **Daniel 9:4-27** – He acknowledged God's character, and asked for mercy and forgiveness. In response, the LORD sent Gabriel to remind Daniel that He loved him. The LORD also revealed significant parts of His plans for the future to Daniel.

13. Habakkuk's prayer in **Habakkuk 3:1-19** – He acknowledged God's works, he asked for mercy, he praised God, he asked questions about God's works, he rejoiced in the LORD, and he acknowledged God's strength in his life.

14. The Lord's Prayer **Matthew 6:9-13** – The ideal prayer. This prayer acknowledged the Father, asks for His will to be done, for today's necessities, for forgiveness, and requests for God's guidance. These are the basics for everyone!

15. Jesus' prayer in Gethsemane **Matthew 26:39-44** When Jesus was facing a terrible death on the cross He asked if possible that the Father would spare Him. Nevertheless**, He gave believers the example that they should always ask that the Father override our wants in favor of His will being done!** (These verses are a very difficult lesson for the name it and claim it crowd!)

16. The Publican's disapproved prayer **Luke 18:10-14** – Sinners should ask for mercy. We are all sinners and stand in need of His mercy and forgiveness especially those who may have been

deceived into thinking that they have not sinned or are in some way better than everyone else.

17. Jesus's prayer on the cross **Luke 23:34** – Jesus asks the Father to forgive the ones who were killing Him. How do I react when someone even slightly abuses me?

18. The thief who died on the cross **Luke 23:42-43** – He asked for Jesus to remember him. It is never too late to pray for forgiveness and mercy as long as you are still alive.

19. Christ's prayer for intercession **John 17:1-26** – Jesus acknowledged the Father and his gift of eternal life for those who ask and trust in Him for forgiveness. It is always appropriate to give the good LORD credit and praise for the things that He is doing and for the things that he has done.

20. Stephen's prayer for his murders **Acts 7:60** – Stephen asks God to forgive the ones who were stoning him. Why do we have such a difficult time forgiving others who have done far less to us?

21. Paul prayed for the Ephesian church in **Ephesians 1:15-23** – He acknowledged the Father, he asks for the strengthening of their faith, and that they would be filled with love, and the fullness of God, he praised God.

22. Paul prays an additional prayer for the Church in **Ephesians 3:14-20**. Here Paul prays for the church to have strength

In these selected prayers several things stand out. First very few of them contain all of the components of the ideal prayer listed in **Matthew 6:9-13**. Most of them acknowledged the Father and some characteristics of Him. Many of them ask for forgiveness and mercy. Some addressed an immediate need. Yet these prayers stand out in the Bible. This leads me to the conclusion that acknowledging the Father is very important. He already knows who He is; so, the important thing is for each of us to embed in our heart the reality of His identity. These prayers are also relatively short. They prayed for what was needed. They were not strangers to prayer. The plea for mercy indicates that they were acknowledging their sinfulness and their need for forgiveness and Devine help.

The believer's lessons from these prayers are evident. Pray for whatever the Spirit quickens you to pray about when He quickens you. And when you pray acknowledge the attribute of the Father that best addresses your need.

## CHAPTER 41

# EXAMPLES OF PRAYERS OFFERED IN OUR ERA

If you have doubts about how the good LORD answers prayers today look up the life of George Muller https://en.wikipedia.org/wiki/George Müller. George Müller was born Johann Georg Ferdinand Müller, 27 September 1805 and died 10 March 1898. He was a Christian pastor and the founder and manager of an orphanage in Bristol, England. He cared for approximately 10,000 orphans, he also educated and provided apprenticeships for them. He was criticized by some who thought that he had elevated the poor orphans above their natural place in English society.[1]

If you were to read further about George Muller you could discover some of the many things that he accomplished by prayer.

**NOTA BENE: HE MADE IT A FIRM POINT TO NEVER TELL ANOTHER HUMAN BEING ABOUT ANYTHING THAT HE NEEDED. HE PRAYED DIRECTLY TO THE GOOD LORD AND THE LORD PROVIDED.[2]**

He was best known for the orphanage that he founded. He met all of the orphans needs by prayer alone. He also founded and funded the Scriptural Knowledge Institute. For this need he received by prayer £ 500,000. This organization distributed Bibles and funded some 200 missionaries.[3] All of these needs were provided by prayer alone. He never solicited funds.

On one occasion it was time for breakfast. There was no food in the orphan's home. The children were seated at the tables with empty bowls before them. George bowed his head and said the blessing thanking God for the food they were about to eat. As he finished praying there was a knock on the door. It was a baker who said that he couldn't sleep and that he had a strong feeling that the orphans needed some bread. He got up at 2:00 AM and baked bread for them. As soon as he finished talking there was another knock on the door. It was a man who was delivering milk. His cart had just broken and he was wondering if they could use the milk since he had to unload it in order to repair his wagon. That morning the orphans had fresh bread and fresh milk and a spiritual lesson that I doubt they would never forget.[3]

Another time he was on a ship going to a speaking engagement. The sea was very foggy. He was concerned the he might be late for his sermon. He had never been late before. He asked the Captain if they could go somewhere and pray for the fog to lift. They went to a nearby room and George prayed. The captain started to pray and George said it wasn't necessary. They went on deck and saw that the fog had lifted and the ship was near land.[4]

Or read about Trans World Radio, a missionary radio station. Go to: _www.twrbonaire.com/about/history_[6]

TWR was enabled to establish a missionary radio station in Tangier, Morocco. This is near the Strait of Gibraltar. TWR also constructed a very powerful short wave radio station on the island of Bonaire, South America in 1964 to transmit the gospel into Latin America. I heard a missionary give testimony about some of the things the good LORD did so that they could transmit the gospel to people who had never heard about Jesus. He said that one time they purchased a transmitter on credit. The contract stated that if they didn't make each payment on time they would lose everything that they had paid and forfeit the transmitter. One month the offerings were severely down. They were short of the required amount. The day before the money was due they asked their banker how much money they had in their account. It was not enough. The missionaries prayed. The next day they went to the bank, they had no more money. They asked the banker to check just one more time. The banker came back excited. Overnight the Deutsche Mark had suddenly risen and the value of their money had increased enough for them to make the payment. God is good!

I had a recent and less dramatic answer to prayer. I was feeling poorly. I had tried a mail-order probiotic and it seemed to help a little. It was 10-20 times a strong as the ones you normally find in a drug store. It was a Sunday afternoon and I was feeling miserable. Nevertheless, Wolfgang needed to go for his afternoon walk. I had put it off as long as I could. It was near sunset. It also looked like it was about to rain. As I walked I prayed. I asked the LORD to help me with this problem. I had decided to make this a short walk. When we got to the turn-around point I saw a friend. We chatted for a few minutes and his wife came outside. She asked me if I could wait for a couple of minutes. When she returned she gave me some information about an extra special probiotic that was twice as strong as the supper one I was taking. Monday morning when the stores were open I went and asked for the probiotic that she mentioned. They had an equivalent one in stock. I bought it and placed it in my refrigerator. I promptly started taking it. It helped significantly with a problem that I had suffered with for two months. **Thank You Jesus!** The LORD often answerers prayers in ways that we couldn't anticipate.

After you check out what the LORD has done through and for these believers ask yourself: "Why am I so ignorant of what the LORD is doing in this day and time and what is He wanting to do through me?" He is still doing miracles! Many Christians, sadly, are not giving Him the credit that He deserves! If a person fails to ask for His Devine help when he desperately needs it, is he in effect denying the power of God?

# CHAPTER 42

# SOMEONE ELSE'S PRE-WRITTEN PRAYERS

### Prayers are not poetry!

Prewritten prayers are similar to training wheels on a child's bicycle. They are for beginners and people who need to upgrade their prayer life. A good prewritten prayer can serve as a guideline or framework for a believer to help raise his prayer life into a better relationship with the Father. Constant dependence upon someone else's prayers can move a Christian toward stagnation in his spiritual growth. Use prewritten prayers for inspiration. Search out and read the Scriptures that they are based on. The prayers that are recorded in the Genova edition of the Bible are a very good starting place. Treat these prayers as study guides. They are prayers that very devout believers have prayed in the past. Let them help you become more devout. Note their piety! How do you measure up? Do you personally know anyone at their spiritual level? Piety is a spiritual objective that each of us needs to work on regularly!

A pre-written prayer only becomes your prayer only when you mean every word of it in your heart. Just reciting someone else's prayer does not give you any better standing with the Almighty!

It is best to pray honest prayers that come directly from your heart as you are led by the Holy Spirit. The good LORD is not impressed by your grammar or eloquence or with the language you speak. He made you and He knows your every thought! Yes, even the bad ones!

It is a very common weakness for humans to think that prayer consist of special words and pronouncements that cause or at least motivate the All Knowing, All Wise, Almighty God to respond to the request of the one's who most skillfully uses them. Being redundant, I repeat, prayers are not magic words! The LORD looks at the heart. He knows whether or not you or I believe what we are saying. He is not impressed by skillful human utterances.

The LORD is concerned about the condition of our hearts. How holy are we? Holiness is always a choice. Once the decision to become holy is made the God's Spirit will empower your resolve to be holy. The LORD does not force holiness on anyone, but He does offer wonderful incentives that will last forever.

# CHAPTER 43

# MUSICAL PRAYERS

Take a good look through a hymnal. Many hymns are in fact very well written prayers. Some even end with "AMEN". When you sing them and when you mean what they say, you are truly praying to the Good LORD. Sometimes when I am in bed trying to go to sleep I sing some of them in my spirit. It is a good way of extending my evening prayers. Normally these prayers fade into restful sleep.

One time when I was a member of a church in east Texas It was prayer meeting night. I was there on time. However, the lights were out. A motorist had an accident and had taken out a utility pole. Two members who lived close by brought their Coleman lanterns. They lit up the room sufficiently. The pastor led the singing. One of the songs he chose was "Send The Light". As we sang the first stanza the lights came on. The volume and enthusiasm increased instantly. We sang all four verses. The good LORD does answer musical prayers!

Listed below are a few samples of the prayers contained in some hymns of the faith. I have chosen hymns that have been around for many years for various reasons. First of all, I believe their thoughts are more devout. Secondly, by now their copyrights have expired.

**All of these hymns are in "The Baptist Hymnal" copyrighted in 1883.**

"All hail the power of Jesus name"- A praise hymn that acknowledges Christ

"All the way my Saviour Leads me"- A prayer that acknowledges Jesus' guidance

"Bless be the tie that binds"- A prayer for unity among believers

"Friend of sinners, hear my plea"- A prayer for forgiveness

"Guide me, O thou great Jehovah"- A prayer for guidance

"Heal me, O my Saviour, heal"- A prayer for healing

"I am thine, O LORD"- A prayer of dedication

"Jesus keep me near the cross"- A prayer for spiritual strength

"Oh for a thousand tongues to sing"- A prayer of praise

"Pass me not, O gentle savior"- A prayer requesting the privilege of service

"Rescue the perishing"- A prayer for the salvation of the lost

"Saviour, like a shepherd Lead us"- A prayer for guidance

The list of prayers in Christian hymnals is almost endless. When you sing or hear others sing hymns, let them be the prayers of your heart. If you have a problem with their content then you probably have a problem acknowledging your own sins. If you see the word "blood" and it offends you, then you need to go back to the starting point. The blood of Jesus is most precious. If you think otherwise, then you are either severely backslidden or unsaved and deceived by Satan into thinking that you are a Christian. It is better to find out now than to later discover your lack of relationship with the Father when it is too late.

This in my opinion is the best musical prayer of all times.

https://www.youtube.com/watch?v=SXh7JR9oKVE

# CHAPTER 44

# PRAYER GUIDELINES

**Confess your faults to one another,
and pray one for another, that ye may
be healed. The effectual fervent prayer
of a righteous man availeth much"**

James 5:16KJV

**"and whatever we ask we receive from
him, because we Keep his commandments
and do what pleases him."**

I John 3:22

Constantly keep in mind that as a believer God is your loving Father. He knows everything past, present and future. He expects us to share our needs and concerns with Him. Because He loves us and knows everything, we should trust Him to choose the best outcomes for us. Many of these things are so wonderful that as mere humans we can't understand or fully comprehend them. Simply trust Him. **ALWAYS ASK FOR HIS WILL TO BE DONE IN EVERY REQUEST!**

Think about the early Israelites who thought that they were doomed when they had the Red Sea on one side and Pharaoh's army rushing toward them on the other side. They didn't know enough to ask God to part the sea and let them through and drown the Egyptian army in the mist of the sea. Moses only told the people to:

**"...Fear ye not, stand still, and see
the salvation of the LORD,...."**

Exodus 14:13a KJV

The LORD did much more than any of them (including Moses) could have possibly anticipated. Always trust the LORD and ask that His will is done. You too may someday stand with your mouth wide open in amazement. He loves each of us very much! He demonstrates it for us every day. Look for his hand at work in your life. It is always near.

George Muller recognized these guidelines for successful prayer. In the Book "George Muller Delighted in God" it cites his method for having successful prayers.

1. We should pray that God's will is done in every request. (**I John 5:14**)

2. We should remember that none of us has earned special standing with the Good LORD. Our connection with the Father is only through the name of Jesus (**John 14:13** and **14**). Muller emphasized the consequences of harboring sin and not seeking God's forgiveness (see verse **Psalm 66:18KJV**): "**If I regard iniquity in my heart, the LORD will not hear me.**" If we hold on to our sins and not seek forgiveness and escape from them, our prayers **will not** be heard.

3. Believers must have faith that God will do the things that He said He would do. In **Mark 11:24**, it says, "**...whatever you ask in prayer, believe that you have received it, and it will be yours.**"[7]

> **It is significant to note that in his lifetime George Muller read the entire Bible approximately 200 times and meditated on it daily. He knew the Word!**[8]

By prayer alone, George Muller received **£ 1,453,513 13s 3d for the support of the orphanage he founded.**[9] In current 2020 U.S dollars this calculates to **$429,072,099.00**[12]. Nearly a half billion dollars was provided by one man's prayers and a God that loved him and the work that he was doing. This is not to mention the vast sums of money he raised for The Spiritual Knowledge Institute, The various schools he supported and the many other Christ honoring works that we will not find out about until we see him in Heaven.

George Muller, a devout student of the Holy Scriptures had a four-part suggestion for those who wanted to increase their faith:

1. Read the word carefully and meditate on what it says.
2. Don't commit sins or do anything not in line with the good LORD.
3. Don't recoil from any spiritual challenge that the LORD gives you.
4. Patiently allow the LORD to work.[11]

He depended 100% on the LORD. The LORD delivered whatever was needed, when it was needed.

Should you be moved by the Holy Spirit to do something in obedience to the Good LORD and your heart is right with Him, then there is no reasonable way you can claim that you didn't have sufficient financial resources to do His will.

**"....ask and ye shall receive, that
your joy may be full."**

John 16:24bKJV

# CHAPTER 45

# YOUR PRAYER SCORECARD

This chapter is written to promote introspection and motivate improvements in your prayer life. It's aim is to help you make the spiritual decisions that in the future you will be happy that you made. First of all, stop and think for a few minutes. What percentage of your prayers have been clearly answered? You prayed for safety in a dangerous situation and you were spared harm. You were sick and you are now well. You were going on a journey and prayed for safety and you traveled without any harm. You had an argument with someone and he is now your friend.

Believers pray for many things and they seldom stop and appreciate what the Good LORD did for them. On the other hand, some people prayed as hard as they could and the opposite of their request happened. Others didn't choose to pray and haven't bothered to think about the possibilities of outcomes being any different as the result of prayer.

Now, examine the results of the prayers that you have prayed. Are there better outcomes that you could have received? Consider the percentage of your prayers that you believe were positively answered. If you can't think of any or if the few that came to mind are minor events. stop and ask yourself, "Why has the LORD chosen to not answer my prayers?" Be honest with yourself. No one else is involved. Do you want to make improvements? I challenge you to make the changes that you honestly believe are in your own best interest!

Unfortunately, too many of us choose not to seek the assistance of the LORD and end up not having ever participated in anything of lasting spiritual value.

On the other hand, some people do get many favorable positive answers to their prayers. Have you thanked the LORD for his loving care? If not, this is something that you can easily fix. First confess the sin of un-thankfulness to the Father and ask for His forgiveness. Next start thanking Him for his merciful blessings.

Everyone can make improvements in their prayer life. God created each of us for a purpose. When you are doing what you were created to do and be, you will have a more victorious life. You will not regret the decision to firmly place your trust in the Good LORD and seek daily minute by minute to do His will. There is nothing better!

# OTHER CITATIONS

1. https://en.wikipedia.org/wiki/George_Müller
2. George Muller The man of Faith, page 8 Frederick G. Warne, Pickering & Inglis Ltd 1937.
3. George Muller Delighted in God by Rodger Steer, page 244 Harold Shaw Publishers, United Kingdom, 1981.
4. George Muller Delighted in God by Rodger Steer, Harold Shaw Publishers, United Kingdom, 1981. Page 161
5. George Muller Delighted in God by Rodger Steer, Harold Shaw Publishers, United Kingdom, 1981. Page 226-227.
6. Transworld radio page 80 www.twrbonaire.com/about/history.html
7. George Muller Delighted in God by Rodger Steer, Harold Shaw Publishers, United Kingdom, 1981. Page 245.
8. George Muller Man of faith and Miracles, by Basil Miller, Bethany House Publishers, 1941, page 142.
9. George Muller Delighted in God by Rodger Steer, Harold Shaw Publishers, United Kingdom, 1981. Page 302.
10. George Muller Delighted in God by Rodger Steer, Harold Shaw Publishers, United Kingdom, 1981. Page 302.
11. George Muller Delighted in God by Rodger Steer, Harold Shaw Publishers, United Kingdom, 1981. Pages 310-311.
12. Calculated by Michael S. Freeman, my financial advisor.

# SCRIPTURAL INDEX

The Chapter and page columns refer to
this book and not to the Bible.
(Bible verses shown in parenthesis are for
reference. The ones without
brackets are printed out in the chapter that they are cited in.)

# UPCOMING BOOKS IN THIS SERIES

These books are written and are in the fine tuning, proofreading, and editing stages. Hopefully to be published in the near future.

**Praying in God's Will Discussion Guide** – This book is based on the book **Praying in God's Will.** It is a formatted study plan for a guided discussion of the book. The guided discussion format was chosen for several reasons. It allows a busy person the option of leading a Bible study with a minimum of preparation time. Any Christian has the potential of successfully leading a guided discussion Bible study. He or she will quickly learn where each person is spiritually and will be able to see them grow as they become more emersed in the Word. Each chapter is divided into discussion segments of about twenty questions. Most questions have a response for the teacher. At the end of each chapter there is a quick reference listing of the Scriptures that are used in **Praying In God's Will**. It lists the page number in the text and the verse that is cited in the discussion.

**"Praying in God's Will - Discussion Guide for Parents"** – This book is a companion book to **"Praying in God's Will"**. It also contains the full content of **"Praying in God's Will - Discussion Guide"** The difference is that it also contains considerable additional questions and comments that are geared to helping parents who are concerned with the salvation of their children. (NOTE: If you are 90 years old and your son or daughter are 70, they are still your children!) This study is also applicable to other believers who are very concerned about the salvation of others who are dear to them. These are very tender topics. At times they can be very emotional. It is also an especially vital study. Unfortunately, many have, for various reasons, keep this deeply heart felt need private. It is through sharing our burdens with others who have similar concerns that we gain strength and victory. All of the principals that are in **"Praying in God's Will"** are relevant to praying for dear ones. It is the text book and reference for this discussion guide book.

**God's Will Applications** - This is a practical guide to answering many questions regarding God's will and it also provides the spiritual information and process that apply toward solving several serious problems that a believer could face during his lifetime. In one's life time there are many serious problems that people normally face. These are listed in the order that they may occur. Scriptures and practical advice are given so that a person in bad situations can easily find some of the spiritual help that they will desperately need. Hopefully, by learning these principals many undesirable events can be avoided.

**Understanding God's Will** - An overall detailed view of the scope and nature of God's will. God's will is the most important topic in the Universe. Understanding more of it will help the believer to better cooperate with his Heavenly Father. God's will is vast. It is concerned with everything!

**God's Will Discussion Guide**– A series of at least twenty questions per chapter with responses. Anyone who is a believer can lead a guided discussion Bible study by using this format. It is an excellent guide for a group Bible study based on the book "Understanding God's will". It contains much information not covered in "Understanding God's Will". The chapter numbers and topics are the same as those in "Understanding God's Will".

**God's Will at Work** - This book is different from the others as it goes into the workplace. It explains the principles that produce better and more efficiently made products. It shows the reader the proven underlying Biblical principles related to their work. These principles can expand a person's capabilities for getting their job done successfully. Scripture tells the reader to be fruitful. This book tells you how. It illustrates that when properly applied the Holy Bible is a good foundational text book that relates to every important facet of life.

# UPCOMING TOPICS (NOT YET WRITTEN)

**Discovering God's Will for your life**

A detailed study of Spiritual gifts. There are more of them mentioned in the Word than many believers are aware of. There may also be some spiritual gifts that are not directly mentioned in the Word. When you discover the gifts that the LORD gave to you when you became a believer, then you are closer to discovering His general will for your life. When you are confident in knowing why God made you and what He designed you to do, you will be better equipped to discover and do His will.

# ABOUT THE AUTHOR

The author is an engineer. He has a B.S. in Mechanical/Industrial Engineering from LeTourneau University, and has completed many home study Bible courses from Moody Bible Institute. His Job has always been to solve complex problems. Early in his carrier he was assigned the task of writing an instruction manual for a device that a senior engineer had designed. The difficult part of this assignment was that no one knew how to efficiently adjust it. He solved this problem logically and wrote a clear and easy explanation for those who needed to adjust the device.

Today, a basic challenge, that many people have, is an unproductive prayer life. They pray and nothing seems to happen. As circumstances worsen the need for positive result filled prayer becomes even more important. He has studied the Scriptures and has identified many of the problems believers in the past have had. We face the same basic problems today. There is hope, but too many people haven't read the Bible close enough to identify the clear solutions to their seemingly unanswered prayers. This book is written with the firm belief that the Holy Bible is the key instruction manual for life. This is not a feel good book. It contains a logical analysis of Scriptural facts. When anyone follows God's Word, under the guidance of the Holy Spirit, they can reasonably expect noticeable improvements in their prayer life.

Printed in the United States
by Baker & Taylor Publisher Services